Wishing you a long
wonderful life together.
Bishop & Sister Taylor

then comes
MARRIAGE

then comes
MARRIAGE

MARK D. OGLETREE, PH.D.
DOUGLAS E. BRINLEY, PH.D.

Covenant Communications, Inc.

Published by Covenant Communications, Inc.
American Fork, Utah

Printed in Canada
First Printing: April 2005

11 10 09 08 07 06 05   10 9 8 7 6 5 4 3 2 1

ISBN 1-59156-756-4

dedication

To Janie and Geri. Thanks for being our best friends and making marriage more satisfying and fulfilling than we ever dreamed possible in our premarital innocence. You have taught us the meaning of true love. Also to a colleague, Ken Call, who passed away before his time; to Valerie, Kumen, Celeste, and Taylor, we remind you that your husband and father, Ken, was a man who loved and cherished you more than life itself. Ken was once asked the same question that President Boyd K. Packer was asked: "If you could go anywhere in the world and visit any country, where would you want to go?" Ken quoted President Packer's answer: "I would go home." May we all attain this level of happiness and fulfillment in our families.

acknowledgments

We thank family members who were patient with us as we often worked late-night hours and early-morning shifts to compile this volume. We thank colleagues and friends who read the manuscript, especially Matt Cook. We express appreciation to Covenant Communications for their encouragement to bring this sequel to press. Angela Eschler was especially helpful in making this volume more readable and user friendly.

We are, of course, alone responsible for the content herein.

Mark D. Ogletree

Douglas E. Brinley

author's note

This volume is a sequel to *First Comes Love,* our book for engaged couples or those moving toward engagement and marriage. In that volume we help couples to think seriously about what it will take to make a great marriage. We introduce matters every married couple faces. To complement that effort, we now present *Then Comes Marriage* for couples who made it through the initial screening process, have now tied the knot, and are looking for ideas and ways to enhance their present marriage.

However, this book is not just for newly married couples. It is for couples at all stages of the life cycle. In athletics, when things go awry, even the pros have to go back occasionally to the fundamentals: check their swing, club speed, racket grip, foot position, and concentration, and refocus on the elements of success; it is the same with marriage. We must all occasionally stop and evaluate together how we are doing and what we can do to improve or maintain a high level of emotional and physical compatibility. We hope this effort will be as helpful to you married couples as *First Comes Love* is to those looking toward marriage.

TABLE OF CONTENTS

INTRODUCTION

PART ONE

marriage: surviving vs. thriving

PART TWO

differences in marriage

PART THREE

difficulties in marriage

PART FOUR

strengths to marriage

INTRODUCTION

A popular bumper sticker reads, "Marriage—the number one cause of divorce." Unfortunately, this slogan seems to be consistent with other media messages in our society. In a recent magazine, there was an advertisement for an automobile. The headline was: "The sad thing is, it'll probably be the HEALTHIEST RELATIONSHIP of your adult life."[1] We've heard of people *naming* their cars, but the idea of having a soul-satisfying personal relationship with your car—one that is more satisfying than marriage—seems like a sad commentary on our times.

Similarly, a *New York Times* journalist recently attended a wedding reception and reported hearing a relative say of the bride, "She will make a nice *first* wife for Jason."[2] First wife? Do people really go into marriage with so little expectation of lasting happiness? Marriage, the highest and holiest commitment we make in this life, is often treated so trivially. Today, many approach the marriage altar with one eye, if not both, on the exit door.

There are other media myths that seem to convey similar values pertaining to marriage. In a recent cartoon a woman reassured her boyfriend, "Look, I'm not talking about a lifetime commitment—I'm talking about marriage."[3] Whatever happened to lifetime commitments and all that talk about "until death do us part"? These media examples strongly reflect the prevailing attitude in our society that marriage is becoming a *temporary, disposable* association.

Several years ago, Arlie Hochschild wrote in the *New York Times*, "In the new American lifestyle, rootlessness occurs on a global scale. We move not only from one job to another, but from one spouse and sometimes one set of children to the next. We are changing from a society that values employment and marriage to one that values employability and marriageability."[4] Such perspectives have certainly impacted the way society views marriage. Many young people today do not view a husband/wife relationship in a positive light; half of all teenagers agree that it is a good idea for couples to live together before they marry.[5] And for those who do marry for the first time in our culture, they have a 40% to 50% chance of divorcing in the couple's lifetime.[6] In a recent Gallup poll of couples still married, 40% had at one time considered leaving their partners, and another 20% said that they were dissatisfied with their marriage about half the time. Even though the divorce rate has leveled off slightly, we are still in trouble—big trouble.

The saddest thing about divorce is that most of the time, it is unnecessary. Between 55% and 60% of all divorces take place in "low-conflict" marriages—marriages that family experts call "good enough" marriages. Why do couples look to divorce as an early option? We have not managed to lessen the effects of divorce on individuals, especially children. With that in mind, Elder David B. Haight has written:

> The ever-increasing rise in divorce is ample evidence of how acceptable divorce has become as the popular solution to unhappy or "not-quite-up-to-expectation" marriages.

> But no matter how acceptable divorce has become—how quick and easy to obtain—divorce is tragic and painful, not only at the outset, but also in the years to come.

> Divorce can never really be final. How can mothers and fathers really divorce themselves from their own flesh-and-blood children, or from the memories of days and years of shared experiences which have become part of their very lives?

> Divorce rarely occurs without immense emotional, social, and financial upheaval. Most people underestimate

the alienation, bitterness, disruption, and frustration between a divorcing couple, and among their children, friends, and relatives. Some never adjust to the resulting emotional consequences.

Perhaps most tragic of all is that more than 60 percent of all divorces involve children under eighteen years of age. Children of divorce all too often have a higher delinquency rate and less self-confidence, and tend to be more promiscuous and themselves more likely to have unhappy marriages.[7]

Besides the damage Elder Haight listed, family scholars have further documented the devastating effects of divorce on children. Note the following statistics:

- An estimated 25 million children in this country (36%) live without their biological fathers.

- One out of every six children in our nation is a stepchild.

- Boys who grow up in a home without a father are twice as likely to end up in jail.

- Teens in single-parent and stepparent families are twice as likely to use illegal drugs compared with teens in intact, two-parent, married families.

- About four out of ten first marriages end in divorce; 60 percent of those couples have children.[8]

- Children whose parents divorced are increasingly victims of abuse, and they also exhibit more health, behavioral, and emotional problems.

- Academically, children of divorce struggle when compared with children from intact families. They perform more poorly in reading, spelling, and math. They are also more likely to repeat a grade and have higher high school dropout rates and lower rates of college graduation when their parents separate.

- Families with children who were not at a poverty level prior to divorce see their income drop as much as half. In fact, almost 50 percent of divorcing parents move into the poverty level after divorce.

- Religious worship, which has been linked to better health, longer marriages, and better family life, drops after the parents divorce.[9]

Can you see how important healthy marriages are to the health of our social order? A distressing fact regarding divorce is that many couples regret that they divorced in the first place. Of course marriage has its ups and downs. Unfortunately, many individuals choose to bail out when the marriage is on a downswing, not realizing that things will probably improve. This is a lot like getting off a roller coaster after the first ten feet of track because "it doesn't go high enough." Consider this: "Couples who rank in the lowest percentile on marital satisfaction, but who don't divorce, often say they are very happy five years later, while those who divorce[d] do not."[10] In a recent survey in America, 66 percent of those who are presently divorced answered "yes" to the question, "Do you wish you and your ex-spouse had tried harder to work through your differences?" From the results of a study in Australia, one-third of those divorced regretted their decision five years later, and 40% reported that their divorce could have been avoided.[11]

A further tragedy of divorce is that for those who remarry, most of their marriages will end in divorce again. In fact, over 60 percent of all second marriages fail.[12] Therefore, the answer is not necessarily to go out and find greener grass; the answer is to stay at home and water and fertilize your own lawn. Unfortunately, too many Americans today are looking for disposable lawns.

What we have just described is a worldly view of marriage and divorce. We would hope that faithful members of the Lord's Church would not view the sacred commitment of marriage so trivially. For Latter-day Saints, marriage is intended to last not just a lifetime, but forever.

The proclamation on the family from the First Presidency and the Quorum of the Twelve Apostles declares:

> The family is ordained of God. Marriage between man and woman is essential to His eternal plan. Children are entitled to birth within the bonds of matrimony, and to be reared by a father and a mother who honor marital vows with complete fidelity. Happiness in family life is most likely to be achieved when founded upon the teachings of the Lord Jesus Christ. Successful marriages and families are established and maintained on principles of faith, prayer, repentance, forgiveness, respect, love, compassion, work, and wholesome recreational activities. By divine design, fathers are to preside over their families in love and righteousness and are responsible to provide the necessities of life and protection for their families. Mothers are primarily responsible for the nurture of their children. In these sacred responsibilities, fathers and mothers are obligated to help one another as equal partners. Disability, death, or other circumstances may necessitate individual adaptation. Extended families should lend support when needed.

> We warn that individuals who violate covenants of chastity, who abuse spouse or offspring, or who fail to fulfill family responsibilities will one day stand accountable before God. Further, we warn that the disintegration of the family will bring upon individuals, communities, and nations the calamities foretold by ancient and modern prophets.[13]

From reading the proclamation on the family, one cannot conclude that marriage is an impermanent institution with disposable spouses and temporary children. God's prophets are telling us that the family is eternal. We enter marriage to stay married. Unfortunately, Latter-day Saints are not immune to divorce; sadly, we have our share of casualties, though not as many as those without the gospel have. As a people, we try our best to make our marriages work, and for the most part, we do. In fact, the divorce rate for members of the Church who marry in temples is well below the national average. In a 1993 study published in *Demography Journal*, it was reported that members of The Church of Jesus Christ of Latter-day Saints are the least likely of all Americans to divorce. Furthermore, "Only 13 percent of LDS couples have divorced after five years of marriage, compared with 20 percent for religiously homogamist unions among Catholics and Protestants and 27 percent among Jews. However, when a Mormon marries outside his or her denomination, the divorce rate soars to 40 percent—second only to mixed-faith marriages involving a Jewish spouse (42 percent)."[14]

However, while we may think we're "safe" from divorce because of a statistical advantage, that is not the end of the story. As members of the Lord's Church, we are not merely about *not* getting divorced. There is more to marriage than just survival. You don't hear people at church saying over the pulpit, "Hey, I may be inconsiderate, and my marriage stinks, but at least I'm not divorced." That's the equivalent of a mother who brags, "At least none of my sons are in prison." We should expect more out of life than that—much, much more, especially out of our marriage relationship. This should be one of the most fulfilling and satisfying experiences in our lifetime.

Members of The Church of Jesus Christ of Latter-day Saints should have incredibly great marriages. The Lord did not intend for us to trudge through marriage like a journey through the desert without a canteen. The Lord expects us to have strong, stable marriages and families so that people in our communities and neighborhoods will be forced to notice. President Harold B. Lee described our duty to the world as follows: "I say to you Latter-day Saint mothers and fathers, if you will rise to the responsibility of teaching your children in the home—priesthood quorums preparing the fathers, the Relief Society the mothers—the day will soon be dawning when the whole world will come to our doors and will say, 'Show us your way that we may walk in your path' (see Micah 4:2)."[15]

To let our light shine and be examples in marriage and family life requires the creation of a happy environment for marriage to blossom. To have a good marriage takes work and effort on the part of both husband and wife. Some people mistakenly suppose that if you just marry the right person, then you would be at the end of your troubles. Newly married couples find out soon enough that even when you and your best friend marry, there will be plenty of work ahead to make the marriage thrive. President Gordon B. Hinckley gave this advice to couples:

> Nurture and cultivate your marriage. Guard it and work to keep it solid and beautiful. Divorce is becoming so common, even rampant, that studies show in a few years half of those now married will be divorced. It is happening, I regret to say, even among some who are sealed in the house of the Lord. Marriage is a contract, it is a compact, it is a union between a man and a woman under the plan of the Almighty. It can be fragile. It requires nurture and very much effort.[16]

Marriage does take effort and nurturing if we want our relationship to thrive and be successful. For those who work at it, there are abundant benefits and blessings. The National Opinion Research Center does an annual survey on the happiness of adults. Married people report being twice as happy (43.5%) as divorced individuals (21%) and individuals who have never married (18.3%).[17] Here are some of the proven benefits:

1. Married people tend to live longer, suffer less from illness, and recover more quickly. They also exhibit fewer risk-taking behaviors and have the lowest rates of suicide and alcoholism.

2. Married people are likely to be happier and enjoy higher well-being in all facets of life. They suffer significantly less from depression and other psychiatric disorders.

3. Married people are usually better off economically, spend less, and save more; two-parent families are a powerful barrier against poverty.

4. Married people are more fulfilled in their sexual relations than other sexually active people. They are less likely to be disinterested in or to feel anxiety over sex.

(These benefits do not extend to cohabiting relationships and apply in lesser degree to remarriages.)[18]

Such benefits come from marriage. Though marriage will not make us immune to trials, it seems to make the ones that come more bearable. We cannot overstate the contribution of marriage to the happiness of individuals, families, and communities.

Nevertheless, the challenge for most Latter-day Saints is not how to survive marriage, but how to enhance, strengthen, and magnify our marriage relationships. President James E. Faust related that "happiness in marriage . . . can exceed a thousand times any other happiness."[19] We believe that this is true. There is nothing more fulfilling than a happy marriage and family life.

The purpose of this book is to assist you to develop a thriving marriage. Our desire has been to write about what makes marriages grow and blossom. We want couples throughout the Church to succeed in marriage. We have relied on scripture, the words of living prophets, research from social scientists and marriage experts, and our own experiences as husbands and fathers. Our hope is that you will read this book together as a couple and discuss the ideas conveyed in each chapter. We believe that if you read the book together and strive to apply the principles and concepts taught, you will gain under-standing and insight into your relationship and you will strengthen your marriage. Remember, President Hinckley said that marriage requires nurturing and effort. Our prayer is that you will give that effort to the most important thing you will do in this life. If you will apply the teachings in this volume to your marriage, you will improve your marriage too so that your "happiness can exceed a thousand times any other happiness."

PART ONE

---

marriage:
surviving vs. thriving

Now, the most important principle I can share: Anchor your life in Jesus Christ, your Redeemer. Make your Eternal Father and his Beloved Son the most important priority in your life—more important than life itself, more important than a beloved companion or children or anyone on earth. Make their will your central desire. Then all that you need for happiness will come to you.

—Richard G. Scott,
"The Power of Correct Principles,"
Ensign, May 1993, 32

CHAPTER 1

keys to a happy and successful marriage

It was President Boyd K. Packer who explained that "true doctrine, understood, changes attitudes and behavior. The study of the doctrines of the gospel will improve behavior quicker than the study of behavior will improve behavior."[1] The doctrines of the gospel can strengthen and enhance marital relationships more than the wisdom of man. With that in mind, consider the following keys to successful marriage as found in the scriptures.

Key 1: Husbands and wives need each other for support, help, and strength.

The scriptures state that "neither is the man without the woman, neither the woman without the man, in the Lord" (1 Cor. 11:11). How true! A man needs a wife, and a woman needs a husband. It would be hard for a husband to reach his full potential without a loving and loyal wife; likewise, a loving and encouraging husband who builds and lifts his wife is a blessing to her. President Joseph F. Smith explained: "No man can be saved and exalted in the kingdom of God without the woman, and no woman can reach perfection and exaltation in the kingdom of God, alone. . . . One is not perfect without the other."[2] More recently, Elder Henry B. Eyring taught: "At the creation of man and woman, unity for them in marriage was not given as hope; it was a command! [see Gen. 2:24]. Our Heavenly Father wants our hearts to be knit together. That union is not simply an ideal. It is a necessity."[3]

Satan would have us believe that marriage is unnecessary, that people could be happier if they would live together either first or indefinitely without the restrictions of marriage. Marriage, he declares, is an archaic institution. He would have us remain alone, focused only on ourselves, believing that we don't need marriage. However, even some of the "wisdom of man" disproves this thinking. Linda Wait, a family scholar from the University of Chicago, documented in her research that married people tend to live longer, have healthier lifestyles, and generally live happier lives.[4] Not only does this research confirm Paul's assertion that men and women need each other and are benefited by the marriage relationship, but that our society also reaps rich rewards when marriages are stable. Marriage produces healthier adults, happier children, and a thriving society.

In addition to producing healthier and happier individuals, a healthy marriage relationship also creates a synergy that cannot be duplicated anyplace else. Where we are weak, our spouse may be strong. Together we can approach the purpose of our creation. A sensitive spouse can help his or her partner learn to be kind, sympathetic, and in tune with the Spirit. A spouse assists his or her partner in becoming more effective as a spouse and parent. Marriage is a profound commitment that we have much to learn about from each other. Together, a man and woman become a great team, with each spouse helping the other overcome weaknesses as they are forced to rely on each other. Let us illustrate the power of this principle by sharing an experience of a colleague and his wife. To protect their identity, we'll call them Derek and Natalie.

Derek and Natalie and their children moved into a new community. Shortly after their arrival, Derek received impressions from the Spirit that he would become the new stake president. He tried to brush the impressions off because he was new in the area and felt he was basically unknown, even though he was serving as the executive secretary. On the day the stake was reorganized, leaders of the stake, members of the high council, bishopric members, and their wives were asked not to leave town. Having convinced himself that he was mistaken, Derek felt comfortable having his wife, a part-time coach, help out with a volleyball game several hours' drive away.

Following Derek's interview with the presiding officer, he again felt prompted. But now, without his wife, he felt a loneliness that he could not describe. He felt that the burden of such a call was overwhelming. As the stake executive secretary, he was required to stay at the church until all of the interviews were completed. As he was walking out the door of the church, the interviewing authority said to him, "Derek, we'll see you this afternoon at 4:00 P.M. at leadership meeting." It was said so casually that he again thought he was mistaken.

At 3:00 P.M. Derek received a phone call from the outgoing stake president, who said, "Derek, the Visiting Authority would like to speak with you and your wife in the stake president's office immediately." Derek's heart sank as he realized that his wife could not be there. He explained to the stake president that his wife was away, and the president asked for her cell phone number so he could call her.

As Derek was driving to the stake center, now deeply humbled and feeling unprepared, he felt the need for Natalie more than ever. He needed her strength and companionship. The General Authority contacted Natalie and informed her of her husband's new Church calling and asked her if she would be supportive of that call. Her answer was, "Of course." Derek was issued the call without Natalie at his side. He felt empty and alone. He wanted to talk with her; he wanted to be reassured by her, but she wasn't there. He was informed that he needed to call two counselors and those names were needed immediately. Derek, because he knew few people in the stake other than the presiding officers, was at a loss as to whom to suggest. He went into a private room to pray but ended up sobbing. He submitted two names, only to have the Presiding Authority turn them down. Apparently they could not be released from their present positions. Derek muttered to himself, "If I could just have my wife here to talk to, I think I could do this." He was granted a little more time, as it was obvious to the Presiding Authority that Derek was struggling with names. Finally, just as the last meeting was to begin, Natalie arrived. After a few minutes with her, being reassured of her support, Derek felt renewed.

When the query again came about counselors, Derek spoke confidently, "I think the Lord would be pleased if we had Brother _____ as the first counselor and Bishop _____ as second counselor." With that decision now made and his wife back with him, he could move forward.

In a later conversation, Derek explained how he'd felt: "Without my wife's help, support, and encouragement, I simply could not function properly."

Elder Richard G. Scott offers this insight:

> In the Lord's plan, it takes two—a man and a woman—to form a whole. . . . For the greatest happiness and productivity in life, both husband and wife are needed. Their efforts interlock and are complementary. Each has individual traits that best fit the role the Lord has defined for happiness as a man or woman. When used as the Lord intends, those capacities allow a married couple to think, act, and rejoice as one—to face challenges together and overcome them as one, to grow in love and understanding, and through temple ordinances to be bound together as one whole, eternally. That is the plan.[5]

Key 2: We should demonstrate kindness and charity to our spouse.

William James, the renowned psychologist, wrote: "The deepest principle of human nature is the craving to be appreciated."[6] These words are a confirmation of the words of an ancient Apostle. In 1 Corinthians 7:3, Paul teaches, "Let the husband render unto the wife due benevolence: and likewise also the wife unto the husband." This scripture is an incentive to avoid selfishness; we can't be so wrapped up in ourselves that we forget to show kindness to our spouse.

Benevolence is demonstrating kindness to each other. No marriage can survive, and certainly can't thrive, without a daily portion of love and kindness. Just as a testimony must be renewed frequently, so faithful married partners need to renew their love for each other on a regular basis. In fact, footnote *c* of this scripture indicates that part of this kindness is shown in continued courtship throughout marriage. Would we not think it odd if a fellow member of the Church bore testimony in this manner: "I haven't had a spiritual experience in twenty years; in fact, I haven't been to church in twenty years, but it's the most important thing in my life." On the contrary, President Howard W. Hunter declared: "A man should always speak to his wife lovingly and kindly, treating her with the utmost respect. Marriage is like a tender flower, brethren, and must be nourished constantly with expressions of love and affection."[7]

We must do more, however, than merely have affection for our spouse. We must show Christlike love. We are to love our spouses as the Savior loves us. Christlike love means to sacrifice and to love someone else more than we love ourselves. Loving our spouse as the Savior loves us comes from the strength and power of His Atonement. True charity involves sacrificing our own needs for those of our spouses.

President Spencer W. Kimball taught that "this kind of love never tires or wanes. It lives on through sickness and sorrow, through prosperity and privation, through accomplishment and disappointment, through time and eternity."[8] The golden rule (Matt. 7:12) teaches that we should treat others the way we want to be treated. There is, however, even a higher law that Christ taught. To borrow a term from the music industry, we like to call it the *platinum rule*, which is found in Matthew 25:40. The rule essentially states that we should treat other people as if they were the Savior Himself. Can you imagine what the divorce rate would be if husbands and wives treated each other as if the other was the Savior? Divorce courts would be empty, and marriage counselors and attorneys would have to seek employment elsewhere.

President Ezra Taft Benson promised, "As you sacrifice for each other and your children, the Lord will bless you, and your commitment to the Lord and your service in His kingdom will be enhanced."[9] President Howard W. Hunter declared: "You are to love your wife as Christ loved the Church and gave himself for it (see Eph. 5:25–31). Tenderness and respect—never selfishness—must be the guiding principles in the intimate relationship between husband and wife. Each partner must be considerate and sensitive to the other's needs and desires."[10] In a recent interview, President Gordon B. Hinckley told the editors of the *Ensign* magazine, "The basis of a good marriage is mutual respect—respect for one another. That is the key. If a husband would think less of himself and more of his wife, we'd have happier homes throughout the Church and throughout the world."[11]

Key 3: A marriage cannot succeed without sacrifice and commitment.

Regarding marriage commitments, a religious commentator recently said on a radio broadcast that "too many people go into marriage with one eye on the exit door." How true that is! We too often are not willing to work at and sacrifice for our relationships. Our world tells us that if it's too hard, we can give up. Contrast this philosophy with an experience Elder Marlin K. Jensen shared:

> Recently, I visited with a widower as he stood bravely at the side of his wife's casket, surrounded by several handsome and stalwart sons. This man and his wife had been married for fifty-three years, during the last six of which she had been seriously ill with a terminal kidney disease. He had provided the 24-hour care she required until his own health was in jeopardy. I expressed my admiration for him and the great love and care he had given his wife. I felt compelled to ask, "How did you do it?"
>
> "It was easy," he replied, when he remembered that fifty-three years earlier, he had knelt at an altar in the temple and made a covenant with the Lord and with his bride. "I wanted to keep it," he said.
>
> In an eternal marriage, the thought of ending what began with a covenant between God and each other simply has little place. When challenges come and our individual weaknesses are revealed, the remedy is to repent, improve, and apologize, not to separate or divorce. When we make covenants with the Lord and our eternal companion, we should do everything in our power to honor the terms.[12]

That is the type of commitment it takes to make a marriage last forever. Such commitment is what our Heavenly Father expects from us; therefore, we should expect it from each other. Not too long ago, a woman wrote about the blessing that type of commitment is:

I was head-over-heels in love with Peter and had been dating him for a couple of weeks when I realized how serious we were both feeling about the relationship. I knew there was something I had to talk to him about, but was afraid—would he leave me? I have multiple sclerosis and had been in and out of a wheelchair already. (I was diagnosed at 18.) I was afraid that once he found out I was "less than perfect" he would leave for someone better. But we sat down together and I told him, knowing the possibilities. He turned to me, held my hand, and looked into my eyes as he said, "Deb, if you are going to be in a wheelchair for the rest of your life, I am going to be there to push it." [From that moment on,] I knew that I would never be with anyone else.[13]

The best answer to today's marriage problems is to stay committed to each other. It will not be easy. We will receive pressure from the world, and pressure from Satan himself, to throw away our covenants and look for happiness in greener pastures. When Elder Jeffrey R. Holland was the president of Brigham Young University, he explained it this way:

Of course some days are going to be more difficult than others, but if you leave the escape hatch in the airplane open because you think even before takeoff you might want to bail out in mid-flight, then I can promise you it's going to be a pretty chilly trip less than fifteen minutes after the plane leaves the ground. Close the door, strap on those seat belts, and give it full throttle. *That's the only way to make a marriage fly.*[14]

If we were to seal the escape hatch and go full throttle ahead in marital relations, never looking back, and yet, of course, adjusting to wind and weather conditions, we would do well. To quote a popular cliché, "Choose your love, and then love your choice." Don't waver. Don't wonder what it would have been like to have married someone else. Don't get caught thinking the grass is greener on the other side of the fence, only to find out later that the grass on the other side may need as much water, fertilizer, and weeding as the lawn you have right now. Those ideas are planted in your minds by the one who would make you most miserable—Satan himself.

Conclusion

Marriage is forever in the Church. Please don't let Satan break your union apart. He will do all in his power to destroy the sacred companionship that began when you made promises in holy precincts. The power that comes to you through ordinances and covenants will see you through some inevitable tight places; we guarantee that some lie just around the corner if they have not yet surprised you.

On the topic of ordinances and covenants saving our marriages, the late Stephen L Richards, as a member of the First Presidency, said, "There never could be a divorce in this Church if the husband and wife were keeping the commandments of God."[15] In a similar vein, President Kimball taught: "When a husband and wife go together frequently to the holy temple, kneel in prayer together in their home with their family, go hand in hand to their religious meetings, keep their lives wholly chaste, mentally and physically, and both are working together for the upbuilding of the kingdom of God, then happiness is at its pinnacle."[16] These are the elements that not only help marriages survive, but make them thrive. Our focus for the remainder of this book will be to better understand marriage and how to not just save it from divorce, but to make it an edifying, fulfilling relationship.

CHAPTER 2

building a marriage on gospel principles

Latter-day Saints are the only religious denomination, Christian or otherwise, who understand that a doctrine of eternal marriage exists, that the union of a husband and wife was not meant to be for this brief mortal span only, but forever. It is a major tenet of LDS theology. When coupled with safeguards that surround a temple marriage—chastity, tithing, the Word of Wisdom, adherence to commandments—the divorce rate of those who so marry is much lower than those who believe that marriage is for this life only. One reason we are a missionary church is to spread the Restoration message that we will continue as male or female in the resurrection. We will not lose feelings for our spouse and children, and a priesthood key restored by Elijah makes eternal marriage possible. When a person believes that marriage lasts beyond this brief time period, he or she possesses a perspective to make marriage and parenthood one of their highest priorities.

Doctrine then, is an important key to developing a long-range marriage. Who knows more about marriage and family matters than Heavenly Father and His Son? Worldly scholars? Philosophers? Those with PhDs trained in the teachings and philosophies of men who know nothing of God's plan of salvation? Within the Church membership, generally those who struggle in marriage are those who are either unfamiliar with this doctrine and its implications or they do not understand their own potential as children of God. In fact, we find that most troubled couples have forgotten the purpose of marriage as it is outlined in the Father's plan. To those with good marriages, knowing that we are in this relationship forever helps us resolve marital problems because we realize that repentance, apologies, and Christlike traits are important keys to the way we treat each other. Humility, meekness, and a desire to be a better companion come from an understanding of who we are and what our potential is as children of God.

Helping the Saints to apply gospel principles to their marriage relationship is the key to marital happiness. One of the problems we all face is that we think we already know the doctrine. But when you spend time with people experiencing marital difficulties, you realize how shallow their understanding is. When we don't understand our eternal potential as a couple, we can become careless in the way we treat each other.

The other problem is that we grow up in a secular educational curriculum that trains us in worldly theories. So when problems arise in marriage, we look first to solutions from secular sources. But educating ourselves via those sources will not empower us as will understanding and appreciating true doctrine.

To know that we had a premortal existence, that we are the literal offspring of Heavenly Parents, that we approved of His plan to come to earth and obtain a physical body that allows us to marry and create children of our own, and that Satan is damned forever for rejecting that plan, helps us keep our marriage on course. From these doctrines we understand such concepts as:

1. In our premortal state, we were unable to marry or be parents.

2. This life, mortality, is our first (and for many it will be their last) opportunity to be a husband or wife, a father or mother.

3. We are apprenticing in marriage and parenthood to see if we can do well, to see if we enjoy these associations.

4. We realize that Jesus Christ made it possible for us to be eternal companions through a resurrection that allows us to remain male and female forever. The Melchizedek Priesthood contains a key to allow us to be sealed as eternal sweethearts in sacred ordinances in Church temples.

5. Spirits, alone, cannot reproduce. It is only when our spirit bodies are united with either a body of mortal flesh or a resurrected, glorified body that we can create offspring.

6. Satan's great damnation, therefore, is that he can never be a husband or father—ever. He wants to make us as miserable as he is. Thus he tempts us to break God's laws and commandments to prevent our being worthy to be eternal companions.

7. We do not want to disqualify ourselves of the privilege of an eternal marriage by the way we behave in our mortal families.

8. Those who do not qualify for eternal lives remain separate and single throughout eternity (see D&C 132:17).

Marriage requires us to continually monitor our behavior so as to comply with the conditions set forth in the doctrine. We must not become careless in the way we treat each other, for our task is to build a relationship that we want to last forever. It doesn't make sense that we could be miserable together in this life but when we die we will be madly in love with each other! We are here on this earth to apprentice in the great opportunity we have to marry and build a companionship that will someday be like that of our Heavenly Parents, for that is our potential.

There is power in this conceptualization. In the proclamation on the family, we are told that we have Heavenly Parents. That means that we have a perfect example of Husband and Father to whom we may go at all times, but especially in times of marital or parenting difficulties. Our Father has been married for a long period of time. We might ask: "Is there a marital problem that God cannot solve?" Of course not, and we have access to Him through individual, couple, and family prayer. And He desires to help us because we are His children. We have a father-son, father-daughter relationship with the most intelligent and experienced Being in the universe. He has indicated that it is His work and glory to help us succeed in this most important stewardship (see Moses 1:39).

The World View Versus the Gospel View

In our contemporary society, marital experts contend that when there is disharmony in a marital relationship, it is probably due to a defect in the couple's communication skills. It is assumed that neither one is listening, speaking openly, or disclosing feelings appropriately. Such experts contend that marital problems arise out of the way messages between spouses are sent and received, misunderstandings between senders and receivers. Once the problem is identified and repaired, it is thought, the couple can get on with their lives.

In researching the subject, we have found plenty of statements from so-called experts in the field of marriage and family relations suggesting that communication issues are the root of marital conflict. However, as we began an effort to square our research findings with what latter-day prophets and Apostles have taught about problems in marriage, we couldn't find a single talk in general conference or any statement by the Brethren that confirmed our scientific research findings. There were no talks on communication, reflective listening, or honest feedback. Instead, what we found were many messages by the Brethren explaining that the root of marital disharmony consisted of selfishness and pride. We also discovered that happy marriages are "most likely to be achieved when founded upon the teachings of the Lord Jesus Christ,"[1] which are in actuality the solution to most marital conflicts.

Nevertheless, many Latter-day Saint wives continue to express the following: "Our marriage would be so much better if my husband would just learn to communicate." It didn't take long for us to learn that, actually, husbands are good communicators when their self-worth is healthy. When we asked a husband to explain the problem, we noticed the man was quite articulate in logically explaining the problem as he saw it. The same was true with the wife. However, when the couple tried to talk to each other, their communication broke down. What was the problem? It wasn't their ability to communicate. It was their negative emotions that got in the way of their willingness to express themselves honestly. Moreover, we found that most individuals communicated just fine with their colleagues at work, their exercise buddies, and those they served with in church assignments. In fact, if any of these relationships ended tragically in divorce, we were quick to point out, "Watch how well some of these men communicate with new women as they enter the dating scene again." And they did. So it wasn't that the individuals weren't capable of communicating thoughts and feelings with their spouse; the problem was that they didn't feel like communicating with a spouse who was critical, sarcastic, or negative much of the time! Risking true feelings, only to have them stomped on, ridiculed, or put down, does not encourage either a man or a woman to continue to risk. Who wants to continue to share inner thoughts and feelings only to have them rejected or ridiculed? It wasn't that they weren't capable of communicating; it's that they weren't communicating about the real problems or were communicating only negatively. This poor communication was a barrier to treating the real culprit—the selfishness of pride.

We do not wish to imply that there is no such thing as communication problems in marriage. In fact, almost all husbands and wives can benefit from and enhance their marriage relationship by practicing and becoming better communicators, as will be discussed in greater detail later in this book. What we do want to make clear, however, is that communication issues are usually not the root of marital problems. Unfortunately, most couples who come into our offices for counseling would rather be told that there is a little communication problem in their marriage rather than something more severe that would take major time, effort, and sacrifice to work out.

Sometimes couples come back to counseling six months to a year down the road because they never really got to the root of what the problem was. They dealt more with the symptoms than with the actual problem. And frankly, communication issues with couples are usually symptoms of a larger problem.

Softening the Heart

So, yes, communication can be a problem—but it should be considered more as a branch or limb on the tree rather than the root. To get to the root of the problem, husbands and wives need to examine their hearts. We believe that most married couples have heart trouble. That is where most of their problems lie. Medically speaking, there may be nothing wrong, but spiritually speaking, many couples could use some "open-heart surgery." Other marriage partners could at least use a little "angioplasty."

Perhaps the best way to soften our hearts is suggested by Elder Robert E. Wells. To combat our selfish nature of trying to affix the blame for problems on our spouse, he recommends introspection. He says to ask ourselves the same question the Apostles did at the Last Supper when told someone would betray the Savior. "Lord, is it I?"[2] Rather than pointing fingers, they looked to see if they were at fault.

In marriage, this same principle is applied when we ask ourselves, "Is there something I am doing wrong that would make a difference in my relationship with my spouse?" A brief introspection with an open heart will allow us to get to the root. As stated above, we already know what the trouble is; to quote President Kimball: "Every divorce is the result of selfishness on the part of one or the other or both parties to a marriage contract. Someone is thinking of self-comforts, conveniences, freedoms, luxuries, or ease."[3] Furthermore, President Benson added, "Pride is the universal sin. . . . Pride is the great stumbling block to Zion."[4] If pride is the great stumbling block to having a unified people, we would submit that it is also the great stumbling block to having a united marriage.

We believe another weapon Satan uses to destroy marriages is *distraction*. This is a way he masks the selfishness and pride we are trying to avoid. He lures us, like fish, with cultural bait that dazzles us, and we all too often succumb to the temptation to think of ourselves and our wants ahead of our real responsibilities. If he can't get us to *do* something horrible, he will try to keep us self-absorbed enough that we won't realize we're *not* doing some of the good things we should. If Satan cannot get us to commit adultery or to rob a bank, he can certainly still distract us and pull us away from what matters most.

As if you haven't noticed, life is extremely busy. There are many interests that compete for our time. It certainly isn't 1950 anymore, when the family would gather around the fireplace and sing songs each night while drinking Tang. The world has changed. For Latter-day Saints with children and a slew of Church responsibilities, finding a night at home with nothing on the schedule calls for a celebration. Our culture has created a time famine. We are so often either dashing madly out the door to a meeting or rushing our children to a practice, recital, or game, or working, or cleaning, or serving. In addition to family and household obligations, our jobs take up vast amounts of our time. Among other things, having mothers in the workforce has limited family time even more. Mothers just don't have the time they used to have to spend teaching, training, and bonding with their children.

It is not just mothers, however, who are busy. Today our children's activities demand our full attention, and with our own busy schedules, there is not much time left for parent-child time. A Gallup poll reported that 41% of adult Americans said they had too little time to spend with their families.[5] The situation has only gotten worse in the last decade and a half since. Besides family obligations and work commitments, Latter-day Saints also commit large amounts of time to fulfill Church assignments. As we are all aware, there are some Church assignments that can pull us out of our homes two or three nights a week, which can be difficult with all of the other demands on our time.

Between work, children, and church, there often isn't any time left for the person who should matter most—our spouse, the one person we will hopefully spend the eternities with. Satan must grin when he sees good Mormon couples so preoccupied with everything else that they have little time for their marriage relationship. Perhaps this tendency is what inspired one musician to write:

> Are you giving the least to those who matter most?
> Or are you sharing your best with those who really aren't
> that close?
> Well, it's time to turn around,
> And find out where your greatest joys are found.[6]

Truly, it is time to turn around, because the greatest joys in this life are found in the marriage and family relationship. But how? How do we make positive changes in our marriages? It begins with each of us as individuals. As the song declared, a good beginning is to listen to our heart. This takes humility—our antidote to selfishness and pride. We must open our heart to the whisperings of the Spirit and be willing to accept the instruction and correction we receive.

The Process of Change

Once we have softened our heart, we can come to learn of our weaknesses (see Ether 12:27). We can see where we need to change. Once again, the Spirit can help individuals understand what they need to focus on. Such focus, guided by the Spirit, makes strengthening our marriage a spiritual experience. In fact, if individuals want to make permanent and lasting changes in their marriage, the Holy Ghost must be part of the equation. Elder Orson Pratt wrote:

> Without the aid of the Holy Ghost, a person . . . would have but very little power to change his mind, at once, from its habituated course, and to walk in a newness of life. Though his sins may have been cleansed away, yet so great is the force of habit, that he would, without being renewed by the Holy Ghost, be easily overcome, and contaminated again with sin.[7]

It is the Holy Ghost that helps us not only to change, but to stay changed. The ways of the world and quick-fix programs will not yield lasting results. In Helaman 15:7 we read that faith and repentance "bringeth a change of heart." These first principles of the gospel bring this change because they help align us with the Lord. Once we begin to see clearly, the way the Lord would have us see, with His perspective, we will "have no more disposition to do evil, but to do good continually" (Mosiah 5:2). We will have hope that we can become better.

Elder Jeffrey R. Holland has testified:

> The most crucial challenge, once you recognize the seriousness of your mistakes, will be to believe that you can change, that there can be a different you. To disbelieve that is clearly a satanic device designed to discourage and defeat

you. We ought to fall on our knees and thank our Father in heaven that we belong to a church and have grasped a gospel that promises repentance to those who will pay the price. Repentance is not a foreboding word. It is, after faith, the most encouraging word in the Christian vocabulary. Repentance is simply the scriptural invitation for growth and improvement and progress and renewal. You can change! You can be anything you want to be in righteousness.[8]

This change process seems to be great for individuals, but what about for couples? As hearts change, resentment is replaced with genuine compassion for the unrepentant companions; and they feel, for the first time, genuine peace. Perhaps the following experience will illustrate.

I saw this process occur in a young man who came to see me. His wife had left him and gone home to her parents because of their marital difficulties. But instead of telling me about all the things she had done wrong, he spent an entire hour explaining to me what the Lord had taught him in the past few days about himself and what he had done to contribute to the reasons for her leaving.

He told me that for several days after she left he was filled with resentment and self-righteous pride and blamed her for most of their problems. Because of the hardness of his heart, he saw himself as the victim of an unreasonable wife who selfishly refused to give her heart to him or to their marriage. Hadn't he done his very best to cope with her unfair and hostile behavior? Little by little his resentment grew until, caught in a web of rationalization and self-justification, he completely distorted his outlook and was unable to see the truth about himself and his wife.

Then one day he was blessed with a moment of grace and insight. While praying, he began to listen to what the Spirit had to say to him. As he did so, he began to view his wife with compassion and realized that she had simply responded out of her own insecurity and in self-defense. He began to feel sorrowful, and he now missed her. His heart was softened, and he was prompted to sincerely ask the Lord what he should do about his marriage. What he heard was very different from what he had expected.

The Spirit began to flood his mind with recollections of many things he had done to disrupt his relationship with his wife and to make things difficult for her: He had put his two jobs ahead of everything. He had made little effort to take time for her or to help her with her responsibilities. He had made light of her concerns as she tried to communicate her feelings to him about their marriage. He had put friends and athletics and selfish pursuits ahead of her. He had not led out in scripture study, home evening, family prayer, or husband/wife prayer as regularly as he should have. In short, he had neglected her needs and the needs of their marriage and had justified his actions by telling himself that he was pursuing her best interests in the long run.

After receiving this veritable flood of insight, he realized how selfish and neglectful he had been, and he felt deeply sorry. As the truth began to seep into his heart, he began to see a different woman than the one he had made his wife into. He began to see her as he had in days gone by. Now he realized that even though she had responded to him in the same way that he had treated her, he could have prevented the deterioration of their relationship by being more responsible himself. Seeing her as the problem had, itself, been the problem. It became obvious to him that the only person he had any direct control over was himself and that changing himself was his best hope for changing the marriage.

This young man had truly humbled himself, desired to know the real truth, and asked in faith. And then he accepted responsibility for the things the Lord revealed to him. Trusting in the Lord and believing that the Lord would help him, he experienced a mighty change of heart. All of these realizations came to him without the help of a counselor—except the divine counselor, the Holy Ghost.[9]

Five Steps to Change

Each of the crucial steps in the transformation process is mentioned in the above experience. If we want to see change in our marriage relationship, we will have to take a similar course of action. First, we must become humble so that we can begin to see clearly. Once we can see clearly, then the Lord can teach us. But how do we strip ourselves of pride, which so easily obscures our vision? President Ezra Taft Benson answered that question when he taught, "The antidote for pride is humility—meekness, submissiveness (see Alma 7:23)."[10] Similarly, King Benjamin said that we must become as a child, "submissive, meek, humble, patient, full of love, willing to submit to all things" (Mosiah 3:19). If we want to see ourselves, our spouse, and our marriage as the Lord does, we must accept and submit ourselves to His view—even if it means facing our contribution to the problem.

Second, we must have a desire to know the truth and to change ourselves. We, the authors, have learned as teachers, counselors, Church servants, and fathers that if a person is unwilling to change, then there really isn't much that anyone else can do to help, other than pray for a softening of the heart. If a spouse has no desire to change, he or she probably won't. Be careful here not to turn your focus on changing your spouse. The only one you can change is yourself. First, cultivate the desire to change. If a person has a great desire to change, the Lord will "compress" the process, and change and renewal can happen instantly and quickly. On this subject, again, Elder Holland has declared:

> You can change anything you want to change, and you can do it very fast. Another satanic sucker punch is that it

takes years and years and eons of eternity to repent. That's just not true. It takes exactly as long to repent as it takes you to say, "I'll change"—and mean it. Of course there will be problems to work out and restitutions to make. You may well spend—indeed, you had better spend—the rest of your life proving your repentance by its permanence. But change, growth, renewal, and repentance can come for you as instantaneously as they did for Alma and the sons of Mosiah.[11]

Now that we have opened our hearts to the possibility of change and cultivated a desire to change and improve, it's time to learn how and what to change. Our third step is to ask the Lord in faith to reveal unto us our weaknesses (see Ether 12:27). Many of us will be surprised how willing the Lord is to show us what our weaknesses are. It doesn't take long for Him to reveal that information to us. All we have to do is ask. Often such revelations can come through leaders, close friends and family, or even a sensitive spouse. Really, if we want to know how to treat our spouse better, who better to ask than him or her? Again, as with any revelation, this requires an open heart.

What we need to remember is that this type of revelation or information is intended to help us. Through Joseph Smith the Lord revealed this truth to the priesthood of the Church: "And inasmuch as they were humble they might be made strong, and blessed from on high, and receive knowledge from time to time" (D&C 1:28). It is through our humility, our openness, and our desire to be better that we can even receive the instruction for change, leading us to action and our next step.

Fourth, we must accept responsibility for our actions. We cannot stop at opening up to change, building motivation, and learning how to change; we must follow through on what we have learned. We must make the changes revealed to us. Our society has become a blaming one. It has become so easy to pass the buck and blame our genetics and environment for everything that goes wrong in our lives. Even in the Church we hear of cases where someone became offended by someone else and decided never to come back to the fold. Laman and Lemuel had the same genetics, environment, and opportunities that were afforded to Nephi and Sam. However, Nephi and Sam made the right choices because they wanted to, and progressed spiritual "light years" beyond their older brothers. Consider the words of Brigham Young: "If Brother Brigham should take a wrong track and be shut out of the kingdom of heaven, no person will be to blame but Brother Brigham. This will equally apply to every Latter-day Saint. Salvation is an individual operation. I am the only person that can possibly save myself."[12] Indeed, owning up to the problem and taking responsibility for change will bring great peace and happiness in our marriages. We can overcome the blame game and can finally take action to bring ourselves in line with how the Lord would have us be.

Finally, we must trust in the Lord and believe that He will help us. As we will discuss more extensively later on, the marriage relationship should be a triad: our spouse, us, and the Lord. One father wisely taught his son, who was departing for his mission, "Two people can do anything, as long as one of them is the Lord." This promise is equally true in our marriages. If couples would make the Lord a part of their relationship, there would be no challenge they could not overcome, no task they could not accomplish.

Along this line, as marriage counselors, we've noticed that most couples who are struggling in their marriage have discontinued the flow of the Spirit in their lives. They have not asked the Lord to sustain their marriage or to be a part of it. First, they have usually ceased making daily personal and couple prayer a part of their married life, and second, they have discontinued reading the scriptures—together or privately. In fact, when one of the authors, Mark, counseled in Utah for three years, he kept a tally of the LDS couples he visited. For three years, not one couple could say yes to the questions: (1) Are you praying together? and (2) Do you read and study the scriptures?

We do not intend to imply that the study of the scriptures and prayer will solve all of our marital difficulties, but they will help in the process of putting Christ back into the center of our lives and giving us a desire to change our hearts. Prayer is the key that unlocks the door and lets Christ into our lives. The scriptures can also add an extra dimension to the marriage relationship. As we see it, reading the scriptures can help us hear the voice of the Lord. Scripture use assists us in resisting temptation, receiving answers to our prayers, and increasing love in our families. Elder Bruce R. McConkie explained:

I think that people who study the scriptures get a dimension to their life that nobody else gets and that can't be gained in any way except by studying the scriptures. There's an increase in faith and a desire to do what's right and a feeling of inspiration and understanding that comes to people who study the gospel—meaning particularly the standard works—and who ponder the principles, that can't come in any other way.[13]

Is there any married couple that you can think of who cannot use this blessing? Is there any married couple that can afford not to read the scriptures? From the scriptures we can learn the doctrines of the kingdom. And, as mentioned earlier in this chapter, it is the doctrines of the gospel that change us, not the study of behavior.[14]

Indeed, the doctrines of the gospel can strengthen and sustain your present marriage and family relationship. Making the gospel a part of your marriage will prevent many problems from happening in the first place. It is analogous to establishing a fence at the top of the cliff which prevents people from falling off the edge, rather than an ambulance at the bottom to carry them off to the hospital when they land. Fences are cheaper, are easier, and involve much less pain than ambulances—so put up a gospel fence in your marriage.

Putting the Savior at the Center of Your Marriage

When a marriage is built on Jesus Christ and His teachings, it will never fall. When trials come—and they will, as well as disappointments, misunderstandings, misdirected priorities, and parental difficulties—Christ will help see such a marriage through. With Him as the anchor in your life, your marriage will not fail! The Lord wants your marriage to succeed, and He wants to be a partner in that marriage. This is why He commands us to yoke ourselves with Him (see Matt. 11:29). President Howard W. Hunter taught:

In biblical times [a] yoke was a device of great assistance to those who tilled the field. It allowed the strength of a second animal to be linked and coupled with the effort of a single animal, sharing and reducing the heavy labor of the plow or wagon. A burden that was overwhelming or perhaps impossible for one to bear could be equitably and comfortably borne by two bound together with a common yoke. . . . Why face life's burdens alone, Christ asks, or why face them with temporal support that will quickly falter? To the heavy laden it is Christ's yoke . . . the power and peace of standing side by side with a God that will provide the support, balance, and strength to meet our challenges and endure our tasks here in the hardpan field of mortality.[15]

President Hunter's counsel to stand "side by side with a God that will provide . . . support, balance, and strength" is vital for us today. Too many couples in the Church are facing life's burdens alone because Christ is not at the center of their marriage relationship. Couples who do not read scriptures together, or pray, or serve are in essence cutting off the flow of living water. Then they do face life's burdens alone. They are not relying on the Savior for support, help, encouragement, and insight into their marriage.

We can have this support if we strive for it. We must begin by letting the Savior into our lives. On another occasion President Hunter declared that "whatever Jesus lays his hands upon lives. If Jesus lays his hands upon a marriage, it lives. If He is allowed to lay his hands on a family, it lives."[16] We must allow the Savior to touch our lives so that we can live as couples eternally.

To some, it may seem weak to actually need someone else to be involved in a relationship so that it will thrive. But the inverse is actually true; we can only become successful if Christ is the center of our relationship. To need His help is not a sign of weakness, but a source of power and strength. As we have already seen, He is the only way for us to make an eternal marriage successful. Relying on Him shows wisdom. Our Heavenly Father and Jesus Christ want us to succeed and be happy, especially in our marriage. Therefore, They are there for us, if we will but make Them a part.

For those of us who are already members of Christ's Church, His promised blessing to each of us is, "Come unto me, all ye that labour and are heavy laden, and I will give you rest. Take my yoke upon you, and learn of me; for I am meek and lowly in heart: and ye shall find rest unto your souls. For my yoke is easy, and my burden is light" (Matt. 11:28–30).

As we begin to place our burdens upon the Lord, He will bless us, and we will begin to think of other's needs instead of our own. This is what the prophets have referred to as stripping ourselves of pride. Great changes will commence as we start to love our spouses more than we actually love ourselves.

Loving Your Spouse More Than You Love Yourself

Several years ago, President Packer told the following story:

> I recall on one occasion, when I was returning from seminary to my home for lunch, that as I drove in, my wife met me in the driveway. I could tell by the expression on her face that something was wrong. "Cliff has been killed," she said. "They want you to come over." As I hastened around the corner to where Cliff lived with his wife and four sons and his little daughter, I saw Cliff lying in the middle of the highway with a blanket over him. The ambulance was just pulling away with little Colleen. Cliff had been on his way out to the farm and had stopped to cross the street to take little Colleen to her mother who waited on the opposite curb. But the child, as children will, broke from her father's hand and slipped into the street. A large truck was coming. Cliff jumped from the curb and pushed his little daughter from the path of the truck—but he wasn't fast enough.

> A few days later I had the responsibility of talking at the funeral of Cliff and little Colleen. Someone said, "What a terrible waste. Certainly he ought to have stayed on the curb. He knew the child might have died. But he had four sons and a wife to provide for. What a pathetic waste!" And

I estimated that that individual never had had the experience of loving someone more than he loved himself.[17]

Perhaps the tendency to love ourselves first is human nature, and
it is definitely what Satan would have us do. However, the Lord works
differently. We have been taught to "love the Lord thy God with all
thy heart, and with all thy soul, and with all thy mind. This is the
first and great commandment. And the second is like unto it, Thou
shalt love thy neighbour as thyself" (Matt. 22:37–39).

We can learn to love our spouse more than ourselves by putting his
or her needs and desires before our own. In order to do this, we must
make sacrifices. In fact, making sacrifices is how we learn to love
people. You can't truly love someone until you make sacrifices for them,
or in other words, give up something you value—be it time, money, or
even your pride—for them. As one wise individual said, "Only if you
sacrifice for a cause will you love it."[18] Missionaries do not begin to love
their missions until they start sacrificing; most members of the Church
will not enjoy or appreciate a calling until they begin to sacrifice; and
how can parents love their children until they begin to practice the
principle of sacrifice?

Christ gave the Church everything He had. Like Cliff from
President Packer's story, Christ loved the Church members more than
He loved His own self. He loved us all enough that He was willing to
give His life! Do we possess this sacrificial, Christlike love? If we do
not, we need to. We can start by sacrificing for our spouse. There is
something right now that each of us can put on the altar to make the
relationship with our husband or wife more rewarding and fulfilling.
This is what will help us to truly love them. President Benson gave a
great discourse on this topic. (Though he was speaking to men at the
time, the principles of love and sacrifice hold true for women as well.)

He [the Lord] said, "Thou shalt love thy wife with all
thy heart, and shalt cleave unto her and none else" (D&C
42:22). To my knowledge there is only one other thing in
all scripture that we are commanded to love with all our
hearts, and that is God Himself. Think what that means!

This kind of love can be shown for your wives in so many ways. First and foremost, nothing except God Himself takes priority over your wife in your life—not work, not recreation, not hobbies. Your wife is your precious, eternal helpmate—your companion.

What does it mean to love someone with all your heart? It means to love with all your emotional feelings and with all your devotion. Surely, when you love your wife with all your heart, you cannot demean her, criticize her, find fault with her, or abuse her by words, sullen behavior, or actions.

What does it mean to "cleave unto her"? It means to stay close to her, be loyal and faithful to her, to communicate with her, and to express your love for her.

Love means being sensitive to her feelings and needs. She wants to be noticed and treasured. She wants to be told that you view her as lovely and attractive and important to you. Love means putting her welfare and self-esteem as a high priority in your life. . . .

Remember, brethren, love can be nurtured and nourished by little tokens. Flowers on special occasions are wonderful, but so is your willingness to help with the dishes, change diapers, get up with a crying child in the night, and leave the television or the newspaper to help with the dinner. Those are the quiet ways we say "I love you" with our actions. They bring rich dividends for such little effort.[19]

We close with one last lesson on what it means to love our spouses more than we love ourselves. In the 1850s Brigham Young sent the first missionaries to the Hawaiian Islands. At first, their labors were futile, but eventually the missionaries met a person who became the key figure to missionary success in Hawaii—Jonathan H. Napela. With the help of Brother Napela, the missionary work began to flourish. If that was all that we knew about Brother Napela, he would be considered a hero to many Saints in the Islands. But there is so much more that makes this man a hero to all members of the Church. He demonstrated perfectly Paul's admonition for husbands to love their wives even as Christ loved the Church. Elder Yoshihiko Kikuchi explained:

> In 1873, Kitty, the wife of this great man, Jonathan Napela, contracted leprosy. She was a beautiful and noble woman in the early days of the Church in Hawaii. Today modern medical knowledge has advanced so that this disease is no longer fatal, but at that time, there was no cure for this dreadful disease. In order to prevent the spreading of this disease, once you contracted it you were forced to live on the seashores in the leper colony on Molokai. The lepers were taken there by boat. The sailors were so afraid of this disease that they pushed the patients into the sea, forcing them to swim to shore.

> Because his wife had to go to Kalaupapa, the leper colony, Jonathan, too, wanted to go. He took her hand and they went there together. Why would he do this? Because he loved her so much! He knew that life is eternal and love is eternal, even through days of "sickness and health." . . .

> History records that this valiant and giant man of God worked in the leper colony and fought to obtain government assistance for the lepers to have a more comfortable place to live. He was a giant in the pure love of Christ for his own people. . . .

> This good brother later contracted that same disease and died even before his wife passed away. She followed him two years later. Husbands, do you love your wife as a daughter of God? Oh, "husbands, love your wives" as daughters of God, "even as Christ also loved the church, and gave himself for it" (Ephesians 5:25).[20]

To love our spouses as Christ loves us is one of the noblest, most fulfilling endeavors that this life offers. Peace and happiness will fill our lives, and Satan will be bound in our homes.

Conclusion

When we look at marriage through the clarifying lens of the gospel, we can see the real problems facing marriage—namely, selfishness and pride—as well as the solutions to these problems. We can recognize the principles of the gospel as they apply to our marriage. Starting with these gospel principles, we become humble, opening our hearts to change. We then build on this humility by following the Spirit and completing the process of change, aligning ourselves with the Savior. Doing so, we come to see that we are not merely building on a foundation of the gospel, but on the Rock, our Savior Himself. This foundation helps us to love as He does, to put our spouse before ourselves. Such love can overcome the challenging differences and needs in marriage.

PART TWO

differences in marriage

*Our differences are the little pinches of salt which
can make the marriage seem sweeter.*

—James E. Faust,
"The Enriching of Marriage,"
Ensign, Nov. 1977, 10

CHAPTER 3

so alike, so different

Have you seen the movie *Sleepless in Seattle?* There is a great scene in the movie where Sam (played by Tom Hanks), his sister Suzy, and her husband Greg are at Sam's house discussing his love life. Sam tells Suzy and Greg that his son, Jonah, called into a national radio talk show and told the host that his dad needed a new wife. As the story continues, a woman named Annie hears the broadcast and consequently wants to meet Sam on top of the Empire State Building on Valentine's Day. As Sam shares this experience, Suzy says, "Oh, it's like the movie *An Affair to Remember*." Suzy then proceeds to describe the movie, and her emotions overtake her. She begins sobbing as she relates the romantic plot of the movie. As she weeps uncontrollably, the men look at each other in disbelief and shrug their shoulders as they wonder what has come over Suzy. After Sam discounts the film as a "chick flick," he and Greg poke fun at Suzy's emotions using a "real man's" movie, *The Dirty Dozen*. As they recount the movie's plot, they sarcastically begin to weep and wail. The scene ends comically as all the characters have a good laugh over their own emotional reactions.

Though relying heavily on exaggerated gender stereotypes, this classic movie scene depicts one major difference between men and women: emotional responses. Most women have probably cried during a movie, while most men probably never have. It's not that women are just a bunch of crybabies; they simply view the world differently. In fact, men and women don't even experience life the same way. To make such statements may seem a little confusing.

Remember, you married your spouse because of all the great things that you had in common. Do you recall when you first met? Perhaps you discovered that you could talk easily together; maybe you seemed to have similar values and beliefs and shared similar opinions; you probably liked the same music; or you learned that your taste in food was similar. However, if you are like most couples, as you progressed through courtship and engagement, differences in personality, character, manners, and habits came to the surface in one way or another. Once they have been married for several years, many couples begin to wonder if they have anything in common at all!

Gender Differences

We would like to address some typical but little-understood differences between men and women. Though these differences are common, keep in mind that they are not necessarily true for every couple in every situation. It is commonly recognized that in studying genders there are more specific differences to be found *among* the groups being compared than *between* the two groups. That is, one woman will vary more from any other woman than all women in general will vary from all men in general. Therefore, our purpose in the next two chapters is not to stereotype or undermine the uniqueness of each individual, nor to define genders entirely. Our purpose here is to help men and women discover their differences and respect them, instead of using them as a wedge to destroy their marriages. Once differences are understood, they can become a source of great strength to the relationship.

Physical Differences

Obviously, men and women are different physically. Hooray! However, there are other physical differences between men and women that most people are not aware of. Dr. Paul Popenoe, founder of the American Institute of Family Relations in Los Angeles, has uncovered some significant data on the physical differences between the sexes:

1. Men and women differ in every cell of their bodies due to the chromosome combinations that make up males and females.

2. Women have a greater constitutional vitality, perhaps because of their chromosome makeup. Females outlive males four to eight years in the United States.

3. Women have a lower metabolism than men.

4. Women differ in skeletal structure. For instance, a woman's first finger is usually longer than her third. Also, girls' teeth do not last as long as boys' teeth.

5. Women have larger stomachs, kidneys, livers, and appendixes but smaller lungs than men.

6. Women have more emotional swings because of menstruation, pregnancy, lactation, and menopause.

7. Women generally have larger active thyroid glands than men, which makes them more resistant to cold and more prone to goiter problems. Because of this, they also have smoother skin and a relatively hairless body. The thyroid gland also produces a layer of subcutaneous fat, which contributes to important elements of personal beauty. A larger thyroid also makes many women more emotionally responsive, causing them to laugh and cry more easily than men.

8. Women's blood contains more water and 20% fewer red blood cells. Consequently, they often tire more easily and are more prone to faint.

9. Women's hearts generally beat more rapidly (80 beats per minute for women; 72 beats per minute for men) and they have lower blood pressure before menopause.

10. Women can generally tolerate or are more comfortable in higher temperatures than men.

11. On the average, men possess 50% more brute strength than women (40% of a man's weight is muscle, contrasted with 23% of a woman's body).[1]

These factors explain a lot. No wonder we don't see more women playing football or more men crying at the movies. Can these differences impact the marital relationship? Certainly they can. Husbands, you need to realize that your wife is not just trying to raise the power bill and make you mad. She is actually cold nine months of the year. Her body was built differently than yours. For example, Elder Jeffrey and Sister Pat Holland shared a bit of humor regarding their physical differences at a Brigham Young University devotional years ago.

> Pat: Do you want to know what I have told him he does that irritates me the most? It is that he walks everywhere in a hurry—first five, then ten, then fifty feet in front of me. I have learned now to just call out and tell him to save me a place when he gets where he's going.

> Jeff: Well, as long as we are telling secrets, do you want to know what irritates me? It is that she is always late and that we are therefore always running to get somewhere, with me, first five, then ten, and then fifty feet in front of her.

> Pat: We have learned to laugh about that a little, and now compromise. I watch the time a bit better, he slows down a stride or two, and we actually touch fingertips about every other bounce.

> Jeff: But we don't have everything worked out yet—like room temperatures. I use to joke about LDS scripturalists who worried about the body temperature of translated beings. I don't joke anymore, because I now worry seriously about my wife's body temperature. She has an electric

blanket on high for eleven months of the year. She suffers hypothermia at the Fourth of July picnic. She thaws out from about 2:00 to 3:30 on the afternoon of August 12; then it's bundle-up time again.

Pat: He ought to talk. He throws the window open every night as if he's Admiral Peary looking for the North Pole. But let someone suggest a little winter morning's jogging and he sounds like a wounded Siberian sheepdog. Mr. Health here can't tie his shoelaces without taking oxygen.[2]

Perhaps some of you have had similar experiences. How different are men and women?

Is it just body temperature and thyroid glands, or is there more to it than that? Consider the following conclusions from Dr. Joyce Brothers:

Are men and women really so different? They are. They really are. I spent months talking to biologists, neurologists, geneticists, research psychiatrists, and psychologists. . . . What I discovered was that men are even more different from women than I had known. Their bodies are different and their minds are different. Men are different from the very composition of their blood to the way their brains develop, which means that they think and experience life differently from women. . . . Women are left-hemisphere [brain] oriented, more verbally adroit. The left hemisphere develops earlier, which gives them an edge in reading and writing. . . . Men use the right hemi-sphere more efficiently than women do. The converse is not true, however. Women do not use the left brain more efficiently than men. The male and female brains are by no means set up as mirror images of each other. What it adds up to is that we are blessed with two different ways of thinking and learning. The male brain is specialized. Men use the right hemisphere when dealing with spatial problems and the left for verbal problems. . . . The female brain is not specialized. Right and left hemisphere work together on a problem. This is possible because in the female brain left-hemisphere abilities are duplicated to some extent in the right hemisphere and right-hemisphere abilities in the left. . . . The ability to zero in on a problem with both hemispheres makes women much more perceptive about people. [This is sometimes called intuition.] They are better at sensing the difference between what people say and what they mean and at picking up the nuances that reveal another person's true feelings.[3]

Aside from these neurological differences within the brain, there are also some chemical differences that impact the different ways men and women behave. Most often men ascribe their behavior to testosterone levels. In reality, there is some truth to that line of reasoning. At the embryonic stage, testosterone is released throughout the body to make females into males (all embryos are female, unless there is a release of testosterone for those who have inherited the Y [male] chromosome), and the fetus begins to develop masculinization. This hormonal bath of testosterone actually changes the brain and alters its structure; the color of the brain changes.

[Moreover] the corpus callosum, which is the rope of nerve fibers that connects the two hemispheres, is made less efficient. This limits the number of electrical transmissions that can flow from one side of the brain to the other, which will have lifelong implications. Later, a man will have to think longer about what he believes—especially about something with an emotional component. He may never fully comprehend it. A woman, on the other hand, will typically be able to access her prior experience from both hemispheres and discern almost instantly how she feels about it.[4]

So, women, this may be the explanation you have been looking for. Most of us men are just brain damaged—that is our problem! Testosterone, by the way, doesn't just affect they way we think. Our tendency to take risks, to be assertive, to be aggressive, to compete, to fight, to argue, to be rough, to be tough, to brag, to enjoy watching cars crash, and to have an insatiable desire to light things on fire and blow things up stems from the hormone testosterone. If it wasn't for that little chemical, most men would just be happy to sit by the fire and sip warm cocoa while reading a novel.

Testosterone is not the only chemical that makes us different. Serotonin is also a factor. Serotonin is a neurotransmitter that carries information from one nerve cell to another. Serotonin soothes emotions and helps us control impulsive behavior. In studies, monkeys with low levels of serotonin made dangerous leaps from branch to branch. Rats with lower levels of serotonin were aggressive and often violent. Perhaps you have already guessed where we are going with this, but women have higher levels of serotonin than men.[5] We will let you make your own conclusions.

Another interesting aspect when comparing the male and female mind, many couples have discovered, is that men seem to have the unique ability to compartmentalize their thoughts. Put another way, it is as if the male mind is made up of hundreds of compartments, so that men can store their experiences and memories separately from each other.

Therefore, during the course of the day, a male can get upset because he received a traffic ticket on his way to work and put that in compartment 1, become frustrated because he lost his PowerPoint presentation on his computer and put that in compartment 2, and engage in a yelling match with his boss and put that in compartment 3; and so it continues throughout the day. In fact, the rest of the day could be horrendous, and the typical American male will continue to file everything away into little compartments. On the drive home from work, he may get a flat tire, only to find out that the spare is flat as well. When he finally makes it home, with black rubber marks all over his clothes and face, he may trip over all of the toys in the yard on his way to the front door, get mad, scream at the kids, and kick the dog. He may then go into his room to take a shower, only to discover that his wife has been doing laundry all day so there is no hot water. What makes men incredibly talented is that, despite a horrific day, by 9:00 P.M. they can still be ready for prime-time romance. It is a source of therapy for them. Women, on the other hand, are just the opposite. They could never get into a romantic mood after a disastrous day like the one described. In their minds, everything is connected and related—there are no compartments. For a woman, what happened this morning is related to what will happen this evening. A woman can still be mad at her husband for something he did during the Christmas celebration of 1995, and that act alone can directly impact their romantic evening ten years later!

Humor aside, for women, life is all connected. For men, events and emotions are less connected. Because of their brain structures, men and women process life's experiences differently; they do not experience life the same way. This is why it is important that husbands and wives talk about (1) what they think, (2) how they feel about certain issues, and (3) why they feel and think the way that they do. We've mentioned that communication skills alone will not save a marriage; communication is not so much the struggle. But it is still vitally important. It is how we gain insight into one another's perspectives so we can deal with the differences that arise. Positive communication is the key to understanding one another. When you communicate about these issues, listening is important. Don't try to change the other person or solve their problems; just listen and gain understanding.

Another key point here is for husbands and wives to realize that these physical differences are real. Husbands, if you're driving down the highway and your wife insists on turning the heater up and you want the air conditioner on, understand that her need for heat is real. You can adjust by rolling the window down or by taking your sweater off. She wants the heat on because she is actually cold, not because she wants to start a fight with you.

At the same time, wives, understand that the reason your husband makes some of the decisions he does is in part because of the way his brain has been designed to work. He isn't trying to be unreasonable or uncaring. He is just doing the best he can with what he's been given.

Emotional Differences

Now let us consider some of the emotional differences between men and women. Again, these explanations are generalizations, and not all will apply to *every* woman or *every* man. One family scholar has identified some of the key emotional differences between the sexes:

1. A woman is an emotional feeler; a man is a logical thinker.

2. For a woman, spoken language is an expression of what she feels; for a man, spoken language is an expression of what he is thinking.

3. Language that is heard by a woman is an emotional experience; language that is heard by a man is simply information received.

4. Women tend to take everything personally; men tend to take things impersonally.

5. Women are interested in all of the nitty-gritty details; men are interested in the principles, the abstract, and the philosophy.

6. Women have a great need for security and roots; men can be nomadic.

7. Women tend to be guilt prone; men tend to be resentful.[6]

Generally, women are inclined to be more personal than men. The female sex has a deeper interest in people and feelings; hence, building relationships is their aspiration. On the contrary, men tend to be preoccupied with practicalities and facts. For instance, when a young child gets injured and comes running to its mother, she will usually respond by taking care of the child, doctoring the wound, and administering some tender, loving care. However, when the same child with the same injury comes to the father, there is an insightful question that must be first asked: "Are you hurt?" (Mind you, there may be blood running down the child's leg.) That inquiry is usually followed by, "How did this happen?" (The chainsaw could be running in the background.) We don't know why, but for some reason men have to know how the injury happened. Perhaps this is because we do not want the same thing to happen to us. After all, if there is a rusty nail somewhere, or a sharp stick, or a booby trap of some kind, we would like to know about it. Typically, men just want "nothing but the facts, ma'am." We are logical and reasonable. We try to keep our emotions under the surface. One man shared the following experience:

> When I was in the fourth grade, my dad received a transfer, and we were going to move from a place that we loved very much. I will never forget the day that we left. All of the women from the neighborhood were in our front yard, hugging each other, crying, and exchanging addresses. Meanwhile, all of the men were gathered around the moving van examining the hydraulic lift on the back of the truck, and wondering how much weight it could lift.

Isn't that typical? Women are emotional "feelers." They connect to each other. Men are more logical and factual. We have emotions, but we often hide them under the guise of discovering how a hydraulic lift works. If you don't believe us, go into a typical Relief Society room on a given Sunday. The women in that room are usually sharing, discussing, perhaps even shedding tears, and talking about issues from childbirth to teenagers, from cough syrup to chemotherapy. Meanwhile, men are in their priesthood meeting often trying to figure out who is supposed to have the lesson that week. Once that is discovered, men will often spend more time spewing out facts and information rather than connecting with each other. This may be why many men in the Church do not know each other that well—we typically do not connect or share personal information.

As mentioned earlier in this chapter, statistically, women generally live longer than men do; perhaps part of this is because most women share their feelings and release stress. And what about the men? We start having high blood pressure and heart attacks at about age forty. Why? Perhaps one reason is all of the stress bottled up inside us. Men, if we will start sharing more of our personal sides, we may add valuable years to our lives.

Women have a knack for connecting and opening up to one another. Have you noticed that women often send each other notes and cards? In fact, there does not need to be a birthday or anniversary for a woman to send a kind note to a friend. Often women will send "just thinking of you" cards. Would a man ever send another man such a card? Comedian Jeff Foxworthy supposed that such a card would say: "Walt, the other day I was out in my driveway and I saw an oil stain that reminded me of your head. Thinking of you, Ned."[7] No, men just don't do things like that.

Many of the relationships men build with other men are based on competition (perhaps testosterone levels are to blame). For instance, if a group of men went bowling or golfing together, they would concentrate on winning. They would keep score to see who wins, and the loser would always have to buy treats for the winners. While eating afterwards, men might brag about their best shots and harass those who had a bad day on the course. This is just a tradition. Women, on the other hand, would applaud each other's successes. Then they would go out to eat together and talk about something totally different.

For example, there probably has never been as great a tennis rivalry as there was during the 1980s with Chris Evert and Martina Navratilova; but off the court, these women were good friends. After matches, they would often call or visit each other. The winner would always console the loser. Often, they would leave each other notes: "Sorry," or "You'll get me next time." Meanwhile, the two great male rivals at the time were Jimmy Connors and John McEnroe. There was no love lost between these two. They would stare each other down and try to intimidate each other before and after a match. There were no cards from Connors saying, "Don't worry, John, you'll beat the tar out of me next time."[8] The competitive drive overpowers the need for connection.

Saying that men and women are different creatures emotionally is understating the facts. It is important to discuss your emotional differences at some point in your marriage and learn to understand and accept these differences. Understand that a company move, an illness, a misfortune, a financial difficulty, a misunderstanding at church, and a myriad of other things will affect you two differently.

Here's our counsel: wives, be patient with your husbands. Just because he isn't expressing himself in the same way that you would doesn't necessarily mean that he doesn't have strong feelings about the matter. Husbands, be patient and understanding with your wives. Sensitivity to their feelings is what they need most.

Verbal Differences

In our counseling visits with couples, many women will often ask something like this: "What happened to the guy I married? During our engagement he was so thoughtful, courteous, and kind. Not only was he a good listener, but a good communicator as well. Before we were married, we used to talk hours into the night. Now that we have been married for a few years, we never talk about anything, and when I try to, he usually responds with a grunt or mumble."

Most women do not understand that men don't need to speak as much as women do. According to marriage and family therapist Gary Smalley, the average man speaks between 12,000 and 15,000 words per day. The average woman speaks about 25,000 words per day.[9] Do you see the crash coming? By the time a husband gets home from work, he has used up all of his words. He's done speaking, and she still has 15,000 left to go! Husbands, buckle your seat belt and hang on—especially if you have small children in the home and most of your wife's conversations have been centered on kid subjects. You know it's bad when a verbally famished woman begins to tell her entire life story to phone solicitors and the Jehovah's Witnesses when they come to the door. That is because most women need conversation, while most men don't need as much.

These patterns can be detected as early as adolescence. When a teenage boy comes home from a night on the town with his friends, or perhaps even from a date, he usually speaks fewer words than a prisoner of war during an interrogation. A mother may ask, "So, Brandon, how was your date?" Brandon may respond by saying, "Fine." Now a mother has no clue in the world what "fine" means. A father will have to interpret. "Honey, what he means is that he had a great time, no one got severely injured, and he didn't have to spend too much money." That's what "fine" is all about. For a teenage girl, the experience would be entirely different. A mother may ask, "Brittany, how was your date?" At that point, the trigger has been "tripped." For the next hour, Brittany will describe her date in vivid detail. She will describe what her date was wearing, who sat where in the car, the conversation that ensued, where they ate, what everyone ordered, who had dessert and who did not, and who acted weird. Meanwhile, the mother is fully engaged in this conversation, asking questions, making comments, and totally connecting to her daughter. Dad, on the other hand, has long since gone to bed. He tried to stay awake for "who sat where in the car," but he just couldn't stay focused. The dialogue between mother and daughter was simply too much.

A few years ago, one of the authors, Mark, was doing premarital counseling with a couple who became engaged the week before. He asked the husband-to-be, "So, how did you ask her to marry you?" The man described how he proposed in about five minutes. Later in the session, Mark asked the future bride the exact same question. You guessed it. It took thirty minutes to hear her version of the exact same story. Women love conversation. They love to share. They love to know about each other's lives. Men talk as a way to share information, and usually it's not much more than that.

So, wives, when your husbands don't talk to you, it's not because they don't like you. It's just because after the initial courtship—where they were gathering and sharing information—they have slipped back into their natural mode of not talking as much.

Most men will need reminders and encouragement to talk, and they need to be rewarded for doing it. Wives, let your husbands know how much you love it when they share their feelings. Let them know how much you appreciate it when they converse with you. On the other hand, husbands, recognize your wife's need to communicate and give her time to share. Open up your own feeling spout as well. When you come home each day, ask her how her day was and then really listen. It may take her a while to share her experiences. That is just fine. Listening to her will bring you both a more satisfying marriage.

Husbands and wives need to remember that language serves different purposes for both men and women.

Problem-Solving Techniques

It is commonly accepted that men are, by nature, problem solvers. That's what they have been "wired" to do. By nature, we like to fix things that are broken, solve problems, and answer questions. Women, on the other hand, like to share their problems with those closest to them. Now, this *sounds* like a great combination, with women wanting to share their problems and men wanting to fix them. There is only one catch: women like to share their problems, but they do not necessarily want their problems solved. Remember, women love conversation; they like to share problems because they love to communicate, but they are not always looking for any answers. They enjoy the catharsis that occurs during the sharing. Sharing their problems is just a way to connect with another person, particularly their spouse. Often, women discover their own solution in the sharing process. More than having someone rush in and try to "fix" the problem, women need someone to acknowledge, sympathize with, and listen to the problem. This is where you come in, men. Listen, comment, share ideas, but don't impatiently force a solution.

Views on Time

One source of dispute for many couples is time. In fact, it has been argued that men and women view time differently. For many men, time is linear. They view time as a straight-line continuum. In a way, men view time as driving down a long highway, with mile markers, roadside stops, and occasional lookout points. In their minds, once they pass through an event, they are done with that chapter or page and check it off their lists. Therefore men can check off mission, school, marriage, birth of baby, first job, and so on. To men, once they pass through an event or an experience, it is completed.

Women, on the other hand, may tend to view time in cycles, rather than linearly. That is, time can be viewed as a spiral instead of a line. Some scholars contend that this tendency is directly connected to the female menstrual cycle. So women see time as a series of events that they go through again, and again, and again. For women, time is a repeated series of events.[10]

Not long ago, a colleague of ours and his wife had their last child. After the baby turned two, the husband was very excited to get rid of all of their baby stuff. Their oldest child was now sixteen, and it was time to move on to the next phase of life. Therefore, he wanted to have a "baby-equipment bonfire" where they burned the crib, the walkers, the strollers, the toys, and all of those baby clothes! What he needed more than anything was a ceremonial bonfire to signify that they were done with the "baby phase" of their lives. The bonfire was a gateway into the next stage of their lives. After all, he and his missionary companions burned their suits in the mission field when they were transferred. To him this ritual was a rite of passage (or at least, a great excuse to play with fire; take your pick).

On the other hand, his wife couldn't believe what she was hearing. How could he burn the baby crib that all of their babies had slept in? To her, that crib was a time capsule of years of wonderful memories. What was this lunatic thinking? Besides, in her mind, within the next several years they would be grandparents. Where would their grandbaby sleep when their children came to visit? Of course, the only place any of her grandbabies would sleep would be in the very crib where her own children had slept. For her, time was cyclical; life was a series of events repeated over and over.

Ways of Dealing with Disagreements

How we handle disagreements can sometimes cause further disagreements. Often when there is friction in a relationship, men like to retreat, where women want to engage and talk about it.[11] This is why when husbands and wives have disagreements, men often like to go on a walk, shoot a few baskets, go on a drive, or just watch *Sports Center*. Women, on the other hand, want to talk about the issues while there is still smoke trailing out of the gun. In this area, women may need to give their husbands time to simmer down and to think logically about the situation. A man can't always deal with a "hot" issue when his and his wife's emotions are out all over the table. This does not mean that he is ignoring his wife or that he doesn't care about the problem. He just needs time to deal with it on his own, and then he can come back and talk about it. Wives, give your husband some space here, and you will be amazed how quickly and accurately problems can be dealt with. Husbands, if your wife is the one in this scenario who needs time to think and process the situation, let her do it. You'll both be better off because of it. Make sure you schedule a time when you can come back to the issue and discuss it later.

Decision-Making Techniques

Decision-making tactics often differ in marriages. Always try to remember this one grand key: men do things and *then* feel them. Women feel things and *then* do them. A man may not know that making a transfer with his company is the right thing to do until he arrives in the new location and works for a few months on his job. On the other hand, a woman may need to know a move is the right thing for her family before she can even function and gear up for life in another city. Men and women work differently and may even receive answers to prayers in a different way. For this reason, wives must understand that it's not that their husbands are not spiritual or do not care what God may think; men need to understand that their wives may need an answer before taking action.

Approaches to Child-Raising

By nature, men and women bring different child-raising traits to the table, so to speak. It is a blessing that there are many differences between the sexes. These differences are not designed to draw us apart, but to complement and strengthen each other. In "The Family: A Proclamation to the World," we read: "By divine design, fathers are to preside over their families in love and righteousness and are responsible to provide the necessities of life and protection for their families. Mothers are primarily responsible for the nurture of their children. In these sacred responsibilities, fathers and mothers are obligated to help one another as equal partners."[12] These differences are vitally important in raising children. By nature, men tend to emphasize play, while women are more prone to caretaking. Men are rough-and-tumble in their approach with their children, while women are more nurturing. Women tend to be more responsive to their children, while men tend to be firm. Women emphasize emotional security in relationships, while men accentuate competition and risk taking.[13] Working as a team, men and women make great parents when these roles are understood. There is no question that we need each other, particularly in the family.

Individual Differences

Some friction in relationships is strictly the result of personal or individual differences. No two people are alike, and often, disagreements are the result. For instance, Elder Joe J. Christensen told the story of a wife who criticized her husband for the way he ate a grapefruit—he peeled it like an orange. In her mind, only derelicts would eat grapefruit like that. She was worried that she would have to spend eternity next to a guy who ate grapefruits like oranges.[14] There are many small differences that couples must contend with—how we eat corn, how we roll the toothpaste tube, how we feel about politics, and a myriad of others that we cannot list.

For example, some spouses have more energy than others. Some are morning people, and some are evening people. Brent Barlow shared the following insight about his relationship with his wife, Susan:

> Basically, I am a morning person. Susan is a night person. About 10:45 P.M. each night I start falling asleep. By 11:00 P.M. I am out . . . cold. You can set your watch by it. Susan, on the other hand, is just picking up steam by the time the 10:00 P.M. news comes on television. Some of her best work and most creative efforts are done between ten and midnight. In the morning, however, something

quite different occurs. I am awake by five or five-thirty each morning. By then, Susan is just midway through her night's rest. And when I wake up, I wake up all at once. So I get out of bed. My wife, on the other hand, wakes up one limb at a time. . . . If we are driving to Southern California, Susan is asleep by the time we reach Payson. Two or three times during the fifteen-hour ride she seems to come out of her ether-like trance and asks something about me wanting her to drive. Before I can say yes, she has fallen back asleep, so I proceed on. About sixty miles from our destination in California, however, something miraculous happens. She becomes readily awake and volunteers to drive "the rest of the way." By that time I am so tired from fourteen hours of driving that I gladly accept. So she completes that last hour of the trip. We arrive at our destination with her looking fresh and relaxed and me passed out with exhaustion, my head tilted back and my mouth open (much to the delight of our children and other curious onlookers when we arrive). Is there any justice in life at all?[15]

This is why some LDS couples have a difficult time reading the scriptures together and praying as couples. He wants to read at 5:30 in the morning like he did on his mission, and she prefers 10:00 at night. Unfortunately, at 5:30 A.M., she is in deep REM sleep, and by 10:00 P.M. he lies in bed and falls asleep in the middle of his own prayer.

What about punctuality? Some families feel they are on time to a church meeting if, when they arrive, the closing prayer has not been pronounced. Other individuals like to be early for church, and some don't mind arriving sometime between the opening announcements and the closing prayer. As a couple, you will have to discuss your views on punctuality if it becomes an issue. Some view tardiness as rudeness and as a way to say, "I don't care." But a tardy person may simply be overly busy or perhaps disorganized and probably wouldn't even be on time for the Second Coming.

Family-of-Origin Differences

Many of the differences that you will deal with as a couple will be due to the fact that you were brought up in different families. This can become a huge source of contention if you are not careful. How you were raised will be the foundation of many of your beliefs and opinions about marriage. For example, when the renowned psychologist Carlfred Broderick was first married, he and his wife had to work through the protocol of how to handle sickness in the home. Most premarital couples do not discuss what happens when you get sick— it's usually not an issue. So, like most of us, the Brodericks learned by trial and error. Carlfred contracted the flu and therefore went to his bed and waited for his new bride to come and fill him full of fruit juice. In Carlfred's house while he was growing up, the sick became the "star of the show" and were given most of the attention. Moreover, according to Carlfred, it was common knowledge that fruit juice was the cure-all for everything. The more ill you were, the more fruit juice you needed. Therefore, in Carlfred's home, the prizes went to those who were the sickliest. Fruit juice, the remote control, a fan, and Vicks VapoRub treatments could make a sick person feel like king for a day. On the contrary, in his wife's home, if you were sick, you were sent to the back corner of the house so no one could hear you moaning and groaning. When you felt better, you could come out of the cave.

Therefore, shortly after Carlfred's marriage, when he became sick for the first time, he lay there moaning and groaning on the floor, waiting for room service. However, these signals didn't register for his wife. She just stepped over him while she vacuumed the room. After waiting to be served for some time, Carlfred finally asked his wife if they were out of juice. She responded by telling him that she thought they had some. Then finally, it clicked. She said, "Oh, you want me to get you some juice—is that it?" Eventually, she came back with a tiny, thimble-sized shot glass full of juice. He later learned that in his wife's house they rarely drank juice and did so in tiny glasses. In his family, juice glasses were the size of Big Gulps, and there was always someone standing there ready to refill at request.[16]

Is there a problem with either of these techniques? No. It is just a different way to solve the same problem. This is why couples need to talk and agree not to be surprised when their partners do things that seem strange. Perhaps your spouse does something a certain way because that is the only way he or she ever saw it done.

Another large difference that comes from family-of-origin practices is that of parenting issues. Some spouses have been raised in families where there was little discipline, or where parents never raised their voices above a reverent whisper, or where there was a healthy dose of affection. What if such a person marries someone who grew up in a family where there were strict rules, yelling, and little affection? There will be issues that will need to be discussed. A healthy attitude is for couples to try to take the best things from both of their families of origin and build on them. Aside from that, they should also incorporate ideas from other sources or families to bless their own children. Even if you marry someone whose family does not belong to the Church, you can still learn things from them. No one has cornered the market on how to turn out successful kids.

Another family-of-origin issue is traditions, such as birthdays and Christmas. Be prepared, because some newly married individuals believe that only their family knows the *true* way to celebrate Christmas. Some families allow a few Christmas presents to be opened on Christmas Eve. Other families may view Christmas Eve present-opening as cheating. There are other issues to work out, such as where to spend Christmas, whether to encourage a belief in Santa Claus, the emphasis on the true meaning, and so forth. In some families, Christmas decorations come out the day after Thanksgiving and stay up through New Year's Day. Other families are comfortable putting up decorations a few weeks before Christmas and taking them down the day after Christmas. Of course, there are those families who just leave their Christmas lights up year round and others who do not decorate at all.

Birthdays are another area where traditions need to be discussed. One of the authors, Mark, learned this the hard way. In his wife's house, there was no such thing as a birth*day*. It was birth*week*. In her family, the birthday child ate their meals from a special plate. There was also a traditional spanking machine, dinner with parents, favorite breakfast, favorite cake, favorite snack, and practically a parade down Main Street. In Mark's family, when it was your birthday, you had a cake and some presents, perhaps went to Chuck E. Cheese's, and received a free coupon for a round of "Goofy-Golf" if you were good that year. The Ogletree birthday process was over in two hours. Of course, when Mark and Janie married and began to celebrate each other's birthdays, Mark had to be taught the "true" practice of birthday celebration. Some traditions are easier to convert to than others, especially when it's *your* birthday! The point is that this and other family-of-origin issues are areas that most couples don't think to talk over before they are married.

Community Differences

Some couples come from extremely different communities. We know of a couple—and we are sure there are many like this—where he came from a tiny town and she came from a huge metropolitan area. His idea of a good time is watching a video and playing some board games because the town he grew up in was about sixty miles from civilization. Her idea of a good time is going shopping at a nice mall and eating out at a nice restaurant. When they were first married, this couple had many discussions about continued courtship after the wedding. It seemed that Damon was perfectly happy to stay home and watch videos, while Teri wanted to get out and do something. Many of their problems stemmed from the fact that they grew up in different communities and learned to enjoy different forms of entertainment. Furthermore, later in their marriage, he wanted to move out into the country and raise their children on some acreage, while she preferred raising their children in the suburbs. They compromised by purchasing a home on some acreage within the city limits. Expect differences in your marriage to arise because of *where* you were raised.

Religious Differences

Many couples reading this book may assume that religion won't be a problem in their marriage. If we marry a member in the temple, problem solved, right? Wrong. Just because you are members of the same faith doesn't mean that you won't have disagreements on how you live your religion. Some people grow up in homes where television viewing is fine on the Sabbath, while others feel that television viewing on the Sabbath is one step from apostasy. Others grow up in homes where drinking caffeinated drinks is acceptable, while others feel that those who drink caffeinated beverages may be violating the Word of Wisdom. Some feel that when you go on vacation, you do not need to attend church; others feel that when you travel, before you locate the hotel you will be staying in, you need to find the nearest chapel. Whatever the differences are, you will need to discuss them. You do not need to feel like you must adopt everything your parents did, pitting your family against your spouse's family. Take the best things from both of your families and develop some traditions of your own.

Differences from Other Couples

When a couple marries, they begin to form a personality as a couple that will be unique to them, just as they as individuals have distinct personalities. Each couple has a unique personality. Don't try to change that, unless it's toxic. Too many couples compare their marriage with those of other couples and feel that they fall short. Don't ever do that. Believe us, everyone has problems. No one has a perfect marriage personality, even though some couples may like you to believe that.

If your marriage works for you and you're happy, don't worry what other couples are doing. Often in marriage counseling we will talk to wives who are frustrated with their husbands because they begin to compare them with other men in the ward. Perhaps a disappointed wife is aware of a husband in the ward who writes his wife poetry; another husband sends his wife love notes in the mail; another takes his wife out on a romantic date every Friday night; and still another always has his arm around his wife in public places. As this woman who has come in for counseling compares her marriage with other marriages that she observes, she is no longer content. Remember, choose your love, and then love your choice. Your spouse is probably doing many great things that others with so-called great marriages are not doing. Yes, there may be a husband who writes poetry for his wife, but he may not help change the baby's diapers, clean the house, and help the kids with their homework. If fact, your husband may not have time to write poetry because he is so busy helping you in other ways. Now, if your husband doesn't write poetry, help with the kids, clean the house, take you on dates, or send you notes in the mail—if he basically forgets that he's a husband—then you may have some serious issues to work on.

Conclusion

All of these characteristics may not be common in every relationship. Interestingly enough, some men possess more of the female traits than their wives do, and vice versa. Women, you may be married to a man who loves to talk and share, while you may, on the other hand, be quieter. That's fine. If it works, don't try to fix it. We must accept the fact that we are different for a reason. We complement each other. Specifically, we need each other's strengths for survival, for success, and for exaltation. The Lord made us different for specific reasons. Where one partner is weak, the other may be strong. Together, we become a whole. Dr. James Dobson explained it this way:

> Consider again the basic tendencies of maleness and femaleness. Because it is the privilege and blessing of women to bear children, they are inclined toward predictability, stability, security, caution, and steadiness. Most of them value friendships and family above accomplishments or opportunities. That is why they often dislike change and resist moving from one city to another. The female temperament lends itself to nurturance, caring, sensitivity, tenderness, and compassion. Those are the precise characteristics needed by their children during the developmental years. Without the softness of femininity, the world would be a more cold, legalistic, and militaristic place.

Men, on the other hand, have been designed for a different role. They value change, opportunity, risk, speculation, and adventure. They are designed to provide for their families physically and to protect them from harm and danger. . . . This is a divine assignment. Men are also ordained in scripture for leadership in their homes, to be expressed within the framework of servanthood. Men are often (but not always) less emotional in a crisis and more confident when challenged. A world without men would be more static and uninteresting. When my father died, Mom said with a tear in her eye, "He brought so much excitement into my life." That characteristic is often attractive to women.[17]

Perhaps this is why Paul wrote, "Neither is the man without the woman, neither the woman without the man, in the Lord" (1 Cor. 11:11). President Kimball observed:

Our Father made men and women dependent on each other for the full flowering of their potential. Because their natures are somewhat different, they can complement each other; because they are in many ways alike, they can understand each other. Let neither envy the other for their differences; let both discern what is superficial and what is beautifully basic in those differences, and act accordingly.[18]

We must learn how to deal with these differences in marriage. We must recognize that we are not the only one in the marriage with ideas and needs. We must overcome the pride that will not allow us to see our spouse for who he or she is, and be willing to appreciate their differences. As we come to understand our differences, we can make these areas strong points in our marriages. Differences can become more than trials to be endured and survived; they are opportunities to grow and thrive together.

CHAPTER 4

meeting marital needs
and love banking

A well-circulated joke starts like this: A farmer and his wife went into town for their yearly medical checkup. After the doctor had completed the examination, he invited the farmer to leave the room so that he could speak with the farmer's wife alone. The doctor then informed the wife that her husband had a very serious disease. The doctor continued, "He must not have any stress in his life. In fact, you will need to do all of his chores and make him three nice meals a day." The farmer's wife began to fidget, but the doctor continued, "You must be available for him and do things with him, such as watch sports. Do not do anything that would upset him. Without this kind of special treatment, he will die."

The wife then asked, "How long will I need to do this for? A week? A month?"

"No," the doctor replied. "You will need to keep this up for at least a year. After that, we'll do another checkup and hopefully clear him with a bill of good health."

Later, on the way home from the clinic, the farmer asked, "What did the doctor tell you?"

His wife replied, "You're going to die."

Perhaps this humorous story reflects the way some individuals feel about meeting their spouse's needs. In this case, the woman selfishly preferred preparing a funeral to putting her husband's needs before her own. Though we recognize that this story is just satire, unfortunately, there are many couples who may actually be this selfish. Another problem many couples face is assuming that their needs are all the same; one may be doing for his or her spouse what he or she needs to have done, rather than what the spouse needs. We cannot say it enough—men and women are different. Therefore, they will have different needs. As you read this chapter and the two that follow, keep this in mind: accepting these differences and turning compromises into marital strengths is what keeps marriages not just alive, but thriving.

A few years ago a couple went to a professional counselor for some marriage counseling. In a particular session with both of them, the marriage counselor was discussing marital needs. He explained that most divorces could be avoided if couples would just learn what each other's needs are, then strive to meet those needs. For a homework assignment, the counselor sent the couple home to have them write down on separate sheets of paper each other's marital needs. That is, the husband was to write down what he thought his wife's needs were, and the wife was to write down her husband's needs as she saw them. They were to bring their lists in the next week and discuss them together with the counselor.

As the counselor explained this exercise, the husband interrupted, "That's easy, I can do that right now." The counselor responded, "Well, I'm sure you can, but I would like you do to it for a homework assignment so you can really put some thought into it." The man insisted, "I don't need homework. I can tell you my wife's needs right now." Finally, the counselor gave in and said, "Okay, what are they?" The man replied, "She *needs* to clean the house. She *needs* to take out the garbage. She *needs* to get the kids ready for school. She *needs* to make the meals. She *needs* to feed the dog."

The counselor did everything he could to keep from laughing out loud. No wonder this marriage was in trouble. At the same time, it was rather sad that this middle-aged man had absolutely no clue what marital needs were all about. He assumed that marital needs were chores his wife *needed* to do, or worse, the things that his wife *needed* to do in order to make *him* happy. Here was selfishness and pride embodied in the man before him. The counselor was not surprised to hear that this couple divorced a few months later.

We have worked with couples over many years and have been surprised ourselves to learn that too many spouses have no clue as to their spouse's marital needs. Unmet needs always precede divorce. On the contrary, couples who can discuss and meet each other's needs will be on the road to successful marriages.

Defining Needs

As human beings, we all have needs. We have a need to be loved, appreciated, valued, and so on. In a marriage, these needs play an important role in our happiness because most of us marry with the anticipation that our individual needs for companionship, emotional and physical intimacy, intellectual stimulation, and so forth will be met. When needs go unfulfilled in marriage, problems develop. The problems arise in the difference between what *is* happening and what *should be* happening,[1] or what one expects out of marriage or a partner and what actually occurs.

When needs are unmet in marriage, rest assured that it can poison the relationship. Needs, however, usually do not remain unmet for a lengthy period of time. Eventually, most people will try to meet their own needs one way or another. In marriage, if a spouse's needs are not being met, that person may seek to meet their needs in some other way—sports, workouts, hobbies, work, same-sex friendships, and sometimes a relationship with someone of the opposite sex. In some cases, unmet needs lead to an affair, and consequently, a loss of family and Church membership and a life of heartache and despair. In almost every case, the consequences of the affair will far outweigh the original problem. An ounce of prevention really is worth a pound of cure.

This is a worst-case scenario; every unmet need does not result in an affair, and unmet needs do not excuse an affair. But unmet needs can cause us to look elsewhere for fulfillment. For instance, a woman who lives with a critical husband may devote more time and hours to a Church calling and have her needs met by complimentary priesthood leaders and youth. Likewise, a husband whose wife is uncharacteristically messy may find himself working longer hours in his office, where he can have peace and order in his chaotic life.

The needs of men and women are unique, and naturally those needs can cause difficulty in adjusting to marriage. A man can have the best intentions to meet his wife's needs, but if he thinks her needs and his needs are the same, he will fail miserably. We often joke about husbands who give their wives golf clubs for birthdays and season football tickets for Christmas. However, there are deeper issues here. For instance, generally speaking, men have a greater need for frequent sexual intimacy in the marriage relationship than women do. If a man thinks his wife wants to be intimate as often as he does, his sexual advances toward his wife could be seen as demands and could potentially damage the marital relationship. Too many women end up thinking that all their husbands care about is sexual intimacy; too many men end up feeling rejected by their wives. This need not be if husbands and wives will learn more about each other's needs.

Meeting needs isn't always easy. In fact, even those of us who work professionally in the field of marriage and family often struggle with this. A few years ago one of the authors, Mark, was speaking at a workshop in northern Utah where he was presenting ideas on marital needs. He told the above story about the husband who had no clue what his wife's real needs were. Since Mark's wife was in the audience at this particular workshop, he thought he would try to impress her. He wanted to show the audience that it could be easy to know what each other's needs are; couples just had to talk about it. He told the audience that his wife needed time to herself just to rejuvenate and that sometimes he needed to take the kids away for several hours so she could recharge her batteries as a wife and mother. He further told the audience how she needed to be courted each week. He also explained how his wife needed him to be the best dad he could possibly be and how she needed him to magnify his callings in church. After he had rattled off more of his wife's marital needs, she raised her hand and said, "So, when do I get these?" Ouch. Sometimes reality is painful. Moreover, there is certainly a distinction between knowing what your spouse needs and actually doing something about it.

If you don't know what your spouse's needs are, or if you do but choose either consciously or unconsciously to ignore those needs, then your marriage may suffer. Some people are surviving their marriages in "quiet desperation,"[2] to borrow a phrase from President Spencer W. Kimball, while others seek happiness in other areas and often in avenues that lead to withdrawal, negligence, or even infidelity.

The Love Bank and Emotional Bank Accounts

So, how do we meet each other's needs? We'll use an analogy here that everyone can relate to—banking. Each one of us has a love bank. It contains different accounts, one for each person we know. Each person that we know makes either deposits or withdrawals whenever we interact with them. Pleasurable interactions create deposits, and painful interactions equal withdrawals. Obviously, some deposits and withdrawals are bigger than others. They can vary in size. According to marriage expert Gary Smalley:

> A deposit is anything positive or security-producing—anything that gives your mate energy. It's a gentle touch, a listening ear, a verbalized "I love you," a fun, shared experience. Temperament, gender, and birth order [and, we would add, personality type] influence one's personal definition of a deposit. Going for long walks in the woods with a spouse may energize an introvert in the same way a houseful of holiday company (entertaining) energizes an extrovert.
>
> A withdrawal is anything sad or negative—anything that drains energy from your mate. It's a harsh word, an unkept promise, being ignored, being hurt, being controlled. The list could be long. Some withdrawals differ from temperament to temperament; something perceived as a withdrawal for one person might be a deposit for another person. But too much control or being absent too much, physically or emotionally, are always major withdrawals.[3]

Unfortunately, there are couples who haven't made deposits in a while, even though their account is still in the black. They still have a few bucks left to spend, so to speak. There are too many contemporary couples who live on marital credit. That is, they are living on past deposits, but they haven't made or received any recent deposits. Eventually, without replenishing, the resources in their own and their spouse's love banks are depleted. They are too busy, or too mad at each other, or too withdrawn, or too distracted to make any new deposits. They pass in the night and may even wave as they notice each other driving down the highway. Perhaps they are too busy serving in the Church or raising children. Perhaps their work is too demanding. For whatever reason, it has been a long time since they have made a worthwhile deposit. Consequently, their marriage has gone stale. Many couples haven't made a real deposit into each other's marital account for a long time. The withdrawals have exceeded the balance. As a result, their marriage is on the verge of being overdrawn. Ultimately, such relationships reach the point of marital bankruptcy. They are on the verge of losing everything, including the account.

Here is the crucial principle of "love banking": deposit more money in the bank than you withdraw every month. Income must exceed outgo. To divorce-proof your marriage, there must be more deposits into your spouse's account than withdrawals. John Gottman recommends that there really ought to be a 5:1 ratio of positive interactions to negative: five deposits to every one withdrawal.[4] Keep in mind, though, that this is not license to "keep score." Doing the dishes five nights a week will not make up for lying once. Our negative actions—withdrawals—ought not to be deliberate or calculated, just as our deposits ought not always be compensatory.

Conclusion

As a couple, do you understand how you're making withdrawals on your spouse? What do you do that could be considered a withdrawal? One man complains that his wife is always late. To him, being punctual is very important. However, he understands that if he goes anywhere with his wife, they are going to be late. It is just a fact of life. Therefore, Sundays are always a hotbed for contention. He would like to arrive at church ten minutes before the service begins. His wife thinks that if you're in the chapel just before the sacrament prayers, you're on time. This husband has calculated that he will spend about one-fourth of his life sitting out in the car waiting for her. Each time his wife is late, she makes a withdrawal from his account. His insensitivity to *why* she is late, his overreaction to her tardiness, and his constant criticism of her are withdrawals from her account. Each couple will need to discuss their deposit and withdrawal slips.

What about deposits? Do you recognize your spouse's needs and, as a result, put "money" in the love account? What do you do that keeps your love account full? For some, it may be kind words and praise. One wife may love notes and phone calls each day. Some men enjoy it when a wife recreates with them or helps them work in the yard. Others love a special touch or a passionate kiss. Some wives may feel like their husbands make deposits when they take out the garbage. Each couple has their own accounting methods, but ultimately, what it comes down to is overcoming the pride that won't let you admit to or even see the other's needs and the selfishness that won't let you fulfill those needs. It is in humility that we can better serve each other.

Take time to discuss how the two of you make deposits and withdrawals from your "marital bank account," and consider these ideas during the next chapters as we go into further detail on some specific needs of men and women in marriage.

CHAPTER 5

men's needs

By now we've established that men and women are very different in their approaches to life. In some ways, these differing approaches arise out of different needs, and in some ways they create different needs. We wish we knew the individual marital needs of every person who reads this book, but we don't. Some men need more compliments than others. Some women need their husbands to provide better in the way of material things, while others get by rather simply. Needs are unique and specific, and that is why it is important for husbands and wives to talk with each other and identify and define each other's needs. We may even need to help each other realize that some needs are actually frivolous and unnecessary. It is in understanding these different needs that we can better love and serve our spouse, making the relationship more vital and fulfilling, rather than stagnant and barely surviving.

So what are these needs exactly? They will vary from couple to couple, but there are some needs that seem to be universal. After twenty years of research and experience in private counseling, Dr. Willard Harley has identified five of the most basic needs for married men and women. In this chapter, we will focus on some of the general needs of men. The list is ranked in the order of importance.

1. Sexual Fulfillment

This is probably not a surprise to you wives. After all, this is one of the topics that you have more than likely discussed together in your marriage for a number of years. Husbands, so it seems, spend much of their married lives trying to persuade, convince, and even "convert" their wife to the notion that they need to have frequent sexual bonding. Harley contends, "The typical wife doesn't understand her husband's deep need for sex any more than the typical husband understands his wife's deep need for affection."[1]

Most men could be enticed to the bedroom almost any time of day for some prime-time romance. Even if they are not feeling well, men have the ability to "play through the pain." Most women are not like that. When women are not feeling well, there will likely be no sexual contact. For women, a healthy sexual relationship is the product of a healthy marital relationship in general. The better the relationship is for her, the more fulfilling the sexual life will be for the couple—because a happy wife is more likely to feel like being intimate. Moreover, for many women, what happens at breakfast, lunch, dinner, and betweentimes is directly and powerfully related to what may happen in the bedroom. On the contrary, for men, what happens between a husband and wife at dinnertime may not have any relationship to or association with what he hopes will happen after the children have been tucked in bed.

Therefore, the sexual issue often causes friction in marriage because men usually want to engage in sexual activity more often than their wives do. This places men in a vulnerable position; some men feel like they're begging all of the time. Others feel like they have no chance of having their sexual needs met in this lifetime. Dr. Harley explains:

> Unfortunately, in many marriages the man finds that putting his trust in this woman has turned into one of the biggest mistakes of his life. He has agreed to limit his sexual experience to a wife who is unwilling to meet that vital need. He finds himself up the proverbial creek without a paddle. If his religious or moral convictions are strong, he may try to make the best of it. Some husbands tough it out, but many cannot. They find sex elsewhere.[2]

Such statements may make men appear shallow, even carnal. Though the need does not excuse infidelity, the truth is that the sexual experience for men is not just physical; it is an emotional, even spiritual connection to their wives. In reality, sexual relations in the marriage is what endears wives to their husbands. Without this intimate contact, men feel distant and unconnected to their wives. Marriage and family scholar Dr. Brent Barlow explained it this way:

> I believe few wives realize the capability of sexuality to help keep their husbands close to them physically, emotionally, and even spiritually. When a husband experiences sexual fulfillment he feels very close to his wife in many ways. Because the sexual urge is so strong and constant in men, a wife should realize the high degree of fulfillment that comes to a husband when she helps him attain sexual satisfaction. . . . On the other hand, I also believe few wives sense the degree of frustration and alienation husbands feel when a wife refuses or ignores his sexual needs and interests. In reality, it is a compliment that he finds her sexually desirable. I believe a wise and loving Heavenly Father has given a wife the gift of sexual intimacy to help her achieve oneness with her husband.[3]

Wives and husbands should discuss this need to determine how this aspect of their marriage can be strengthened. Both wife and husband will need to understand that their sexual needs will be different. By discussing this issue together, couples can come to understand their differing needs. The key is talking about the issue. It is important for each spouse to share his or her feelings about this part of their marriage. Secretly hoping that one spouse can read the other's mind is probably unprofitable.

It needs to be said that there are a number of marriages where the wife has a greater desire for sexual relations than does her husband. Perhaps that is truer today than ever before. But we rarely run across couples where the husband does not meet his wife's sexual needs in terms of sheer frequency. Husbands should therefore be sensitive to their wives when seeking to fulfill their own needs. Perhaps that is the reason why Elder Richard G. Scott said: "There are times, brethren, when you need to restrain those feelings. There are times when you need to allow their full expression. Let the Lord guide you in ways that will enrich your marriage."[4]

2. Recreational Companionship

Part of the reason men get married is for companionship. In some ways, this is why the first marriage, Adam and Eve, came about—so man would not be alone (see Gen. 2:18; Moses 3:18; Abr. 5:14). Men have a need for companionship in all areas of their lives; often wives are supportive in most of these areas—schooling, church service, work, family life, and such—but leave their husbands to themselves when it comes to spare time. Married men need a wife who will recreate with them; men need a wife to be their best friend. They need someone who will join them in their hobbies and activities. Believe it or not, men love it when their wife helps them build fences, paint rooms, and jump-start the car. They also love it when their wife plays racquetball, hits a few golf balls, and watches their favorite professional teams play. In fact, an ideal Saturday for some husbands would be to work in the yard with their wife in the morning, make a nice lunch together, and then sit down and eat it together while they watch a favorite college football team play. For a man, there may be nothing better than having a sandwich in one hand and his other arm around his wife, watching his team. Whether it be sports, music, movies, art, or whatever, husbands like to be able to share what's important and meaningful to them with their wife.

Wives, you can do this! Remember when you were single and dating? You did all of these things. You went to action films, listened to his music, went jogging, hit baseballs at the batting cage, fished, went to the boat show, and even drank Gatorade. After marriage, however, both genders tend to curtail their interests in these areas and renew their own interests.

Couples need to discuss how they can meet each other's needs in this area. There will be some things you can do together, and some you can do separately—as long as you understand each other. It's true that a couple who plays together stays together. So find a few things you like to do together.

3. An Attractive Spouse

Although this need may seem trivial to women, for men, it is important. Men need their wives to look good, to take pride in their appearance, and to do the best with what they have. Sometimes there is a tendency for both men and women, once married, to let their "appearance guard" down a few notches. Remember how before you were married, you would spend hours deciding what to wear before a date? You would ask your roommates if your socks matched your pants, you would brush your teeth three times a day, and you didn't miss a workout. Now look what happened! We don't even care if our socks match each other anymore, much less match our pants. We go to bed for the evening in our sweat pants, with a Breathe Right nasal strip spanning from cheekbone to cheekbone.

A friend of ours who is a marriage and family therapist was recently visiting with a couple. The wife did not understand why her husband never wanted to be sexually involved with her. So, our friend asked the husband point-blank, "Why don't you want to be more passionate with your wife?" The man then revealed that his wife had terrible breath and rarely brushed her teeth. He further shared that she only showered once or twice a week. When she would roll toward his side of the bed for a good-night kiss, he could barely take the stench. The counselor recommended some personal hygiene tips, and we will assume that their love life changed for the better.

Some women may feel that because they have had several children, they are not attractive anymore. In actuality, any man that is worth his salt will feel that the mother of his children is more beautiful now than she was on her wedding day. No matter what your predicament is, or what you have been through, we recommend that you do the best with what you have, and your husband will love you for it.

We would like to present a caution here. Some women may believe that their husband's need to have an attractive spouse is somewhat immature. You may think so, but please realize that his need for you to look good is just as real as your need for affection and communication. It's not that he needs some kind of glamorous trophy wife; *most* men just need to know that their wife still cares. This doesn't mean having to look like a supermodel; it just means trying a little to take care of yourself. When you look good, he feels good. And in fairness, men, this may be significant to your wife too. It may not make the top five on the list of women's needs, but it is important for you both to keep trying for each other. So don't waste your time questioning this need. You both would be better off if you determined how you could best meet it.

Wives, ask your husbands how important it is for you to look good. They may play this question down if they are smart, but it is important to them. Husbands, be prudent here. Once your wives ask you such a question, don't send them to a clinic for plastic surgery. Be kind and sensitive. And again, before you throw any stones, you may want to examine your own appearance. We are amazed at how many men come into our offices complaining about their wife's appearance; while they are ranting about their spouse's figure, their bellies are hanging about four inches over their belts, their hair looks as if a Chia Pet escaped and parked right on their scalp, and they have enough chins for everyone else on their block.

Women, remember, men are not necessarily hoping that you will be Julia Roberts with a testimony. True beauty comes from the inside, but you can and ought to let that beauty show through how you take care of your earthly temple. Attractiveness is doing the best with what you have. Elder Joe J. Christensen declared, "Occasionally, look in a full-length mirror. Certainly we should not become obsessed with how we look, but we should work to improve our physical appearance. . . . The Lord expects us to do the best we can with what he has given us."[5]

4. Domestic Support

The ultimate fantasy for a man is a home life free of stress and worry. After work each day, in his imaginary world, he comes home to an impeccable lawn surrounded by a white picket fence and walks in the front door. There, he is greeted by his wife with a passionate kiss, and his well-behaved, perfect children are singing, "I'm so glad when Daddy comes home." Next, he walks into their immaculate home, and his wife urges him to relax before dinner. He sits in his La-Z-Boy recliner and begins watching *Sports Center,* while his wife rubs his neck and shoulders. Then, the family eats a steak dinner with conversation at the table that is enjoyable and conflict free. Later, the family goes out for a brief trip to the park, after which they come home, and the kids go to bed with a story, song, and prayer—without any complaining. Then he and his wife head into the bedroom and read, talk, and relax for a while, then head off to bed (but not before a passionate and romantic encounter) and go to sleep by 10:00 P.M. Now, most of you women are thinking, *Dream on.*

The first counseling case one of the authors, Mark, had many years ago involved a couple who constantly argued over the way she kept, or didn't keep, the home. The father worked two jobs so his family could live in a nice home. Because his two jobs kept him away from home, he began to resent his large house with its equally large payment. But at least his home was his castle to come home to—not! Every day, after working a twelve- to thirteen-hour day, he would walk into his home and almost gag. You see, according to him, his wife was the messiest woman in the Church. Upon arriving home, he would walk into dirty laundry strewn all throughout the house. In fact, the family couldn't even eat on the kitchen table because of the junk she had piled on it. Dishes were practically overflowing into the street. There was never any dinner made. In a nutshell, this husband felt like he walked into a war zone every evening. This lack of domestic support caused a deep wedge in their relationship. This husband decided that he would work longer hours at the office rather than come home to such chaos. At least his office was neat and orderly, and he had some control of how he kept his work station. He could relax there. Because his wife refused to change and meet this legitimate need that her husband had, their marriage became worse.

Wives, you have a special role in your husband's life. Your support means more than anything, and this is one way to show that support. Jerome Chodorov wrote:

> I'll tell you the real secret of how to stay married. Keep the cave clean. They [husbands] want the cave clean and spotless. Air conditioned, if possible. Sharpen his spear, and stick it in his hand when he goes out in the morning

to spear the bear. And when the bear chases him, console him when he comes home at night. Tell him what a brave man he is. And then hide the spear so he doesn't fall over it and stab himself.[6]

Today, one of the largest causes of family disagreements is household responsibility. It is right up there with finances and sexual relations. Why? Now, more than ever, more women are in the workforce. Nevertheless, the housework needs to be done. The key is for couples to talk, plan, and organize. Don't let household responsibilities become a major source of contention in your marriage. Husbands, you should also chip in here so that your needs may be fulfilled—especially if your wife must extend herself beyond the role of homemaker to working outside the home. Again, this male need can appear shallow, but it has deeper roots. It's not that men need a maid; they need someone who cares and supports them in their efforts to support the family. As with many of his needs, a husband needs to see that his wife still cares about him and is invested in keeping a well-functioning home.

5. Admiration

Most men have a need to be appreciated, admired. This sounds a little egotistical, but it is true. Of course, women have the same need. But in fact, honest admiration may be an important motivator for most men. It is not as negative as it sounds. James Dobson explained:

> When a woman tells a man she thinks he's wonderful, that inspires him to achieve more. He sees himself as capable of handling new responsibilities and perfecting skills far above those of his present level. . . . Admiration not only motivates, it also rewards the husband's existing achievements. When she tells him that she appreciates him for what he has done, it gives him more satisfaction than he receives from his paycheck.[7]

A wife can be a great motivator for her husband. A man's need for admiration can be met as his wife lifts him up, motivates him, and inspires him to greatness. In a sense, she becomes his therapist, his biggest fan, his largest supporter. All too often, this need for admiration goes neglected. Like other needs, when this need goes unfulfilled, the marriage relationship deteriorates.

We want your marriage to succeed. Husbands, do you need to be appreciated? Do you have a need for recognition and approval from your spouse? Most of us do. Does your wife know that? Does she know that you appreciate her acknowledging the good things you do as a husband and father? In your private conversations, it would not be amiss to let your wife know that you appreciate her telling you when you do good things. We all do. Marriage loses its zest if we do not receive a compliment now and then. She needs to know your feelings about this need.

In Luke 2:52, it states that "Jesus increased in wisdom and stature, and in favour with God and man." Individual self-esteem stands on four of the legs identified in this verse: mental, physical, spiritual, and social. Men need to feel mentally capable, socially likeable, physically attractive, and spiritually vital. Wives can reinforce these qualities in their husbands by sincerely complimenting them in these areas.

Wives, how do you show your husband that you admire him? Do you tell him why you admire him? Why you love him? Find out what matters most to him, and praise him in those areas, and genuinely so. For instance, you may often tell him that he does a great job mowing the lawn. That may be well and good, but what he really wanted to hear was that he is an effective father. Make sure your arrows of praise and admiration hit the target he needs.

Every person needs to know that he or she is loved and appreciated. We could probably save most marriages if there were an increase in positive statements of appreciation for what our spouse contributes to our marriage.

Wives, here is an assignment. Do you wish to build up your husband? Do you want to strengthen his resolve to be a better spouse and father? Do you want to make him feel like you are glad you married him? Write him a note and share with him the things that you admire most about him—other than on his birthday or your anniversary. After he reads your personal message of love and appreciation, you'll notice that his feelings for you will increase, as will his desire to be a good husband. Men love to be genuinely complimented by the person they love the most—their own spouse.

Conclusion

We recognize that we have discussed these issues in a manner that relies on stereotypes. We know there are other needs that we have not addressed and realize that sometimes men and women have similar needs. It would be impossible to chronicle all of the needs of your husband, but that is not the point. The point is for you to discuss your husband's needs and learn how you can fulfill them. Listed in this chapter are some suggested starting points for that conversation. We caution against taking this chapter and using it as a checklist. What your husband needs more than any list of characteristics is *you*. He needs you to be the helpmeet that God has ordained you to be (see Abr. 5:14). He needs you to be the comfort that only a woman in your role can be (see D&C 25:5). As wives learn to fulfill their husband's needs, marriage becomes a thing not simply to be endured, but to be enjoyed.

CHAPTER 6

women's needs

Husbands, here is your chance to learn how to nurture your marriage. By meeting your wife's needs, you will see your marriage grow and become more vital. We will again refer to the writings of Willard Harley to make the case for women's needs. Remember that we are talking in generalities here. Not all of these will apply to you, but hopefully many of them will be helpful to you.

1. Affection

Every human needs intimacy on some level. For men, this need is often expressed and met sexually; for women, it is usually met through affection. It isn't that women do not like to be involved sexually with their husbands, but what is more crucial to women is their need for affection. Of course, affection must precede sex, for without that preliminary activity, sex is interpreted as a selfish act within marriage. In our visits with couples, we are prone to hear women say, "He never puts his arm around me," or "He never hugs me," or "Whenever I hug him, he takes that as a cue that I want to have sex—now." For most women, affection symbolizes security, protection, comfort, and approval. When a husband expresses some form of affection to his wife, he is basically saying: "I'll take care of you and protect you. You are important to me. I'm concerned about the problems you face, and I'm with you."[1]

Consider the concern that one newly married woman shared regarding her sex life with her husband:

Sexual intercourse enabled us to express our love in a new, exciting, and complete way. At the same time, I found that while we expressed our love more physically, we shared less nonsexually. Intimacy outside of sexual intercourse was pushed back several notches, and not for the better. Although I enjoyed and understood the need for the sexual side of our relationship, I began to realize [the lack of] the other sharing we had done before we were married. All of a sudden, I didn't feel that Joe found talking and sharing important anymore, whereas I did. I still wanted and needed to share my thoughts and feelings, dreams and fears with him. There seemed to be a time for love-making but not time for sharing in any other way. I felt his needs were being met but mine weren't.

I also began to realize that the sexual relationship was more fulfilling for me when I felt closer to Joe in other areas of our relationship as well. That "intimacy," while of less importance to Joe's fulfillment, definitely enhanced the quality of my own sexual fulfillment because it provided a sharing and caring that included and transcended the physical realm of matrimony. When I didn't feel appreciated outside the sexual dimension of our relationship, I didn't feel special, unique, or loved. Instead, I felt like just another "thing" in Joe's life. I needed more from our relationship than that. I didn't want to replace or eliminate our love-making, but, rather, blend my needs with his. Over the years we've learned that sexual intercourse isn't really love-making when one or both spouses don't feel loved and respected in all areas of his or her life.[2]

Perhaps this insight helps explain why we need to address women's needs and how husbands can show wives the affection that they require. First, it is important that a wife conveys that information to her husband: "What I need from you to meet my needs for emotional and physical intimacy." It will be different for different women, of course, but there are some forms of affection common to all women. Husbands, wives like nonsexual physical attention—perhaps a hug every morning before you leave the house and an embrace after you walk in the door. Make it a conscious thing to do it and it will become automatic in time. Send her a note or call her on the phone to let her know you have been thinking about her. Help out with the housekeeping chores. We are fairly certain that no husband in America has ever been shot while doing the dishes. Have you ever sent her a love letter in the mail? You can never go wrong with flowers. And you need not wait for Valentine's Day or your anniversary. Surprise her with her favorite flower today. Invite her to go to dinner, formally. That is, ask her on a date, just like you did when you were engaged or dating her. Call her from work and ask her out. You plan it all out, including the babysitter. She may be shocked, but why not? Go on a walk after dinner and hold hands. Don't talk about the kids unless she brings them up; talk about your dreams and what you love about her. When you get home, give her a back or foot rub with no strings attached.

Some men feel that engaging in such romantic efforts is "playing a game." Once you punch all of the right tickets, you get your prize. In fact, some men refuse to carry on this "dramatic display of affection," as they call it. "Why can't women just be sexual, like us?" they whine. One marriage expert explained that a "man who growls, 'I am not the affectionate type,' while reaching for his wife's body to satisfy his desires for sex, is like a salesman who tries to close a deal by saying, 'I'm not the friendly type—sign here jerk . . . I've got another appointment waiting.'"[3]

Men need to meet their wife's need for affection. A wife's need for an affectionate relationship is just as real and legitimate as is a husband's desire to engage sexually. If you can meet your wife's affection needs, it will be more natural, then, for her to reciprocate sexually. This exchange requires each to meet the needs of the spouse if the marriage is to be successful and fulfilling.

2. Conversation

Just as men need recreational companions, women need someone to talk to, someone to share their life with. One of the most frequent complaints from women is, "Why won't my husband talk to me?" At the same time, some husbands are perplexed and wonder, "Why does my wife place such a high priority on communication?" The answer: for women, communication is the key to loving and feeling loved. Women want to share their lives with a spouse who loves them for who they are. They want to grow old with a husband who values them and understands them and who can share their deepest feelings and needs. Women expect love to last forever, and such a relationship is often attained by couples who have learned to reach the deepest levels of human intimacy[4]—physical, mental, spiritual, and emotional.

Men and women view communication differently, and the spoken language serves a different function for each gender. According to one study, men prefer to discuss things like music, current events, and sports. Women, according to the same study, opt to discuss issues like relationship problems, family health, reproductive concerns, weight, food, and clothing. Put another way, men prefer to talk about things outside of themselves, while most women would prefer to discuss topics of a more personal nature.[5]

This need for emotional intimacy affects a surprising number of areas. For instance, often when a man returns home from a trip, the first thing he will want to do is get the kids tucked in bed so that he can be alone with his wife for a romantic evening. At the same time, women who haven't seen their husbands for some time may not feel like lovemaking. They would rather talk in order to reconnect with their husbands. Many women married to men who travel often express how hard it is adjusting to their spouse's return. One said, "It takes a day or two for me to feel close enough to make love."[6] Wives feel more of a need to visit, to talk, and to reconnect with their husband. Once that has taken place, then romance seems more appealing to her.

Along these lines, Dr. Willard Harley recommends that men should devote at least fifteen hours a week to listening to their wife and spending time in conversation with her. This doesn't mean using a stopwatch and tallying the hours. It means quite the opposite, actually. It means not looking at the clock every five minutes while she is talking to you. It means giving a good amount of time each day to your wife, telling her about your feelings, ideas, and problems, and listening to hers. To husbands this may sound difficult, but recall that you did it easily before and after you were engaged to your wife. That's why she felt so drawn to you, so close to you, and so connected. Husbands, when your wife wants to communicate with you, focus on her even more intently than you would your boss. Give her your time and full attention. Don't walk around the house eating snacks and looking for the remote control while your wife is trying to share the meaning of the universe with you. Sit down on the couch, look her right in the eye, and listen to what she wants to say. Occasionally, you may want to restate some of her ideas so she knows you are really listening. Resist the temptation to criticize her or to resolve her concerns. Just listen. If she does share a problem, ask, "Honey, what do you think we ought to do about this? What are some of your ideas?" Practice attentive listening. It is one of the great gifts you can give your spouse.

3. Honesty and Openness

Mere communication is not enough to keep a marriage afloat. There must be trust. Husbands, your wives need you to be honest and open. Without this type of communication, a husband can undermine his wife's trust and destroy her security. President N. Eldon Tanner once said:

> Just imagine the reversal that would take place if full integrity were to rule in family life. There would be complete fidelity. Husbands would be faithful to wives, and wives to husbands. There would be no living in adulterous relationships in lieu of marriage. Homes would abound in love; children and parents would have respect for one another. . . . [How else will our children come to] value honesty and integrity?[7]

To feel secure, a wife must trust her husband to give her accurate information about his activities. A wife needs to feel secure that when her husband says he's running off to a Church meeting or a business trip, that's where he is. She needs to know, when he works in an office full of women, that he maintains discretion in his relationships with them; she should never feel insecure about her spouse's relationships with other women.

According to Bell, Daly, and Gonzalez, the old-fashioned virtues of honesty, trust, and fidelity are still important elements for the success of contemporary marriages. Sincerity, truthfulness, faithfulness, and trust are the cement that binds people together.[8] Wouldn't it be great if every woman could say, as one young wife commented:

> I never have to worry about my husband. When he tells me something I know it's true. He's a very sincere, upfront person. I know where I stand with him all the time. He always keeps his word. If he promises the kids something, he never disappoints them. He travels a lot, but I trust him completely. I know he's faithful to me. He isn't the kind of man to sneak around. If two people can't believe in one another, or depend on one another, they don't have much of a relationship in my opinion.[9]

Such openness and honesty are vital to the trust in every marriage. It means more than husbands sharing their schedule with their wife; it means sharing everything. Husbands, your wife doesn't need any new surprises or revelations—she got a big enough one when she married you. Your wife ought to not only know when you have a meeting or appointment, but she ought to know what the gist of your conversation with the bishop was all about, what you plan for your future together, why you make the decisions you do. Share with your sweetheart. It will pay great dividends for both of you. Perhaps Elder Marion D. Hanks said it best: "Marriage is an everyday and every-way relationship in which honesty and character and shared convictions and objectives and views about finances and family and lifestyle are more important than moonlight and music and an attractive profile."[10]

4. Financial Support

Along with the emotional security we've discussed in the last few sections, women need physical, temporal security. Women need to know there is money in the bank. They need to feel that they can go buy groceries and not bounce a check; that they can buy birthday gifts for their children and not have their husband erupt like Mount St. Helens; that Christmas, "the most wonderful time of the year," won't cause him to have a cardiac arrest. We know that money, or the lack thereof, has been defined as one of the biggest marital problems that leads to divorce. Several years ago the American Bar Association linked 89% of all divorces to quarrels and accusations over money.[11] President N. Eldon Tanner said it this way: "Overindulgence and poor money management place a heavy strain on marriage relationships. Most marital problems, it seems, originate from economic roots—either insufficient income to sustain the family, or mismanagement of the income as earned."[12]

Several years ago a couple came into one of our offices for counseling. The wife was deeply distraught. She and her husband had been married only a few months when she noticed some glaring red flags. About a month after their marriage, all of her husband's ambitions to make money seemed to dissipate. He began to reveal his true character. His idea of a day's work was to put in a full two hours at the office and then come home and watch TV all day. Meanwhile, his wife was working long hours, slaving away as she struggled to make ends meet. She tried to deal with this for a while, but her husband's lack of drive was causing her great distress. They were in debt, and bill collectors were calling regularly. This didn't seem to faze the husband one bit. She began to spend more hours at work so they could meet their obligations. He didn't do anything more to help or solve the problem. The more she pushed, the more he relaxed. To her, debt was unacceptable. She took it upon herself to get the family out of debt. Meanwhile, her husband sat back and watched even more ESPN. For him, life didn't get any better. He could sit home all day, eat junk food, and watch TV while his wife worked. This was the life! She came to realize that her husband was really using her so he could do what he had wanted to do all along—stay home and be a slug. The couple ended up divorcing after only a year of marriage.

Do women marry men for their money? In some ways, yes. Women who want to have a family have the right to expect their husbands to be financially supportive. This idea is not just offered by social scientists. In "The Family: A Proclamation to the World" we read, "By divine design, fathers [husbands] are . . . responsible to provide the necessities of life and protection for their families."[13] If women want to eat with utensils instead of their hands and live in a house rather than a cardboard box under a bridge, they should consider marrying someone with a little cash and the ability to produce some. Indeed, women had better marry someone who will pay the bills and provide for their family. Often, when this financial need isn't met, women head to the workforce to supplement their family income. Contrary to what most people think, however, most married women resent having to work. In fact, most women would love to stay home with their children while their husband provides for the family.[14] Can you imagine the heartache and struggle that many women experience as they leave their young children with day-care providers while they drive off to work?

There are several things that men should do to meet their wife's needs in this area. For one, couples could prepare a budget and live by it religiously. Some couples find it helpful to have separate checking accounts if they cannot agree on how to allocate money. This system requires a monthly balancing to ensure that neither husband nor wife is extravagant or a spendthrift. Each pay period, a certain amount of money is transferred into each spouse's check register, or account, and he or she is free to manage a side of the home expenses. Each month, reconciliation is needed to make sure you and the bank are still in love with each other. But one thing is certain: women don't like to feel like they have to beg for money any more than husbands want to beg for sexual intimacy. Women should be equal partners in decisions about money.

Husbands, if you do not make enough money to meet your financial needs, you have two options: spend less or earn more. It is possible to increase your earning power with an advanced degree or a part-time job. You can also free up more of your current income by concentrating on decreasing your debts. We are aware of a family who paid off their mortgage by delivering newspapers every morning. They did it together for ten years and paid off their home. Perhaps an even greater blessing was that the family learned how to cooperate, as well as learning the value of work and income.

Another solution is, as we said above, to live on less than you earn. You may have to nix the hundred-dollar-a-month hair appointments, the fake baking, and the satellite dish, not to mention the SUV or XBox. When it comes to money and marriage, less may be more.

5. Family Commitment

Finally, amidst all these needs and concerns, a woman needs to know that her husband loves being married and being a father. It is also an added bonus when a wife knows and understands that her husband doesn't mind spending some leisure time with their extended families.

Most wives want their husband to take a leadership role in the family and commit themselves to the moral and educational development of their children. They want their husband to play a key part in training and bringing up the children. Women want a husband who will honor his priesthood and who will preside in the home. This doesn't mean they want their husband to dominate; they just want him to be an appropriate role model for the children. A woman doesn't want a father who watches family life from the sidelines; she wants a quarterback who is involved in every play. This is a legitimate need that women have. Elder Neal A. Maxwell made it clear when he stated, "Even marvelous mothers cannot fully compensate for malfunctioning fathers."[15]

Family science research has documented over the last several years the importance of strong, involved fathers and how such fathers contribute to the well-being of their children. Fathers make a significant difference when they are involved in the lives of their children. Children with involved fathers do better academically, emotionally, spiritually, and socially. Mothers intuitively know that their children need strong, stable fathers.

Men, your wife needs you to be a family man. There are so many things you can do to meet you wife's needs in this area, such as ensuring that you are home to eat meals with the family, going for walks or bike rides together, attending church as a family, conducting family meetings, hanging out with the children, taking an interest in their schoolwork and helping them with their homework, driving car pools, reading to the children before bedtime, working on family projects, having fun together, and a host of other possibilities. You might even ask your wife, "Honey, what can I do to be more involved with the family? What can I do to be a better father? How can I be a better husband?" Get out a note-pad and a pen, and write everything down that she says you need to do. Review it often and implement her suggestions. You will notice a drastic improvement in your marriage relationship.

President Ezra Taft Benson declared:

> As the patriarch in your home, you have a serious responsibility to assume leadership in working with your children. You must help create a home where the Spirit of the Lord can abide. Your place is to give direction to all family life. You should take an active part in establishing family rules and discipline. Your homes should be havens of peace and joy for your family. Surely no child should fear his own father—especially a priesthood father. A father's duty is to make his home a place of happiness and joy. He cannot do this when there is bickering, quarreling, contention, or unrighteous behavior. The powerful effect of righteous fathers in setting an example, disciplining and training, nurturing and loving is vital to the spiritual welfare of children.[16]

In a similar tone, President Howard W. Hunter said, "One of the greatest things a father can do for his children is to love their mother."[17] Husbands can meet their wife's needs in the area of family commitment by rededicating themselves as husbands and fathers and by spending time in each of these areas.

Conclusion

As we mentioned in the last chapter, what a person needs more than anything is the commitment of his or her spouse. Husbands, your wife needs *you;* she needs you to love her, to revere her, to cherish her. As you treat her with such love, you will be amazed at how natural it will be for you to meet her needs. She will flourish under such care.

We don't want to give you the impression that the needs we have discussed in these chapters are the only needs that men and women have. We have simply mentioned a few of the primary ones. You and your spouse will surely have other needs that we have not addressed here. Yet, there is the key. You two need to talk about your needs and be unafraid to share your real, positive feelings with each other. We hope you will talk about them together.

The first step in meeting each other's needs is to talk about them openly and thoroughly and be clear and specific about how you will go about meeting each other's needs. These conversations require humility on both sides. That culprit of destruction, pride, does not let us see how we can change for the better. But in humility, when a spouse gives specific suggestions on how his or her needs can be met, it is possible for the other spouse to understand how to use his or her agency to meet that need. It is when couples play "guess what I would really like to have you do for me" that the problems come. Don't leave any room for guessing here. Wives, if you want your need for affection to be met by your husband, then you must give him specific suggestions on how he can meet that need. Likewise, men, if you need a recreational companion, teach your wife precisely what you need in this area.

Meeting each other's needs requires selflessness on the part of each spouse. It will require you to make sacrifices of time and resources occasionally and to actually place your spouse's needs above your own. It can be done. It's a matter of talking together and making joint commitments that you will do it. It's time to take your marriage out of "survival mode" and give it a chance to grow.

PART THREE

difficulties in marriage

It all comes back to one word, doesn't it: Selfishness.

—Spencer W. Kimball,
Teachings of Spencer W. Kimball
(Salt Lake City: Bookcraft, 1982), 313

CHAPTER 7

dealing with anger

Aside from the differences in genders and differences in individual needs, there are other influences that heavily affect our marriages. One such weapon we unwittingly wield against our own marriages and families is unmanaged, out-of-control anger. We seem to live in a society that is, as Elder Jeffrey R. Holland termed it, angry, armed, and dangerous.[1] News reports incessantly document incidents of rage, abuse, adult temper tantrums, and even murder. Do any of the following headlines sound familiar? "Parents Break Out in Brawl at Little-League Baseball Game"; "Motorist Shoots Another in Dispute over Lane Change." Each time we hear of such tragedies, we feel that we cannot be shocked anymore. And then something even more insane than the last episode follows. For example, a few years ago at a little-league hockey practice in the Boston area, one father actually beat another father to death while several of the boys watched in horror. Ironically, the irate "hockey dad," who was convicted of manslaughter, was upset that the practice was getting too rough.[2]

Consider another example that borders on the ludicrous. In 1988 the *Journal of the American Medical Association* reported on a new illness: "Vending Machine Madness." The article reported that fifteen serious injuries and three deaths had occurred when individuals became extremely irate because the vending machines they were using had taken their money without yielding their coveted soda pop. Consequently, they took out their frustrations on a five-hundred-pound metal box. Each of the "victims" who was killed had rocked the machine so hard in trying to get money back that the machine had fallen on top of them and crushed them to death.[3] Perhaps it would have been more rational for these victims to have left their money in the machine and walked away slowly.

Thankfully, not everyone in our society is trying to maul or maim each other. No, most people prefer the "civilized" manner of getting their point across, like using hand gestures and verbal assaults. We hear often about drive-by shootings, but what is probably more common today are drive-by *shoutings*, as "road rage" continues to be the cause of many highway accidents. In a poll conducted by the American Automobile Association, it was reported that 48% of Americans listed "aggressive drivers" as their chief worry while driving, compared with only 28% who identified drunk drivers as their primary concern.[4] What is becoming of our society? No wonder a popular bumper sticker reads: "If you're not outraged, you're not paying attention."

Anger, however, is not merely a societal ill, or even a global trend. The root of anger too often strikes close to home; in fact, it strikes *in* our homes. Several years ago, President Gordon B. Hinckley commented on what he felt was the most pressing issue concerning the membership of the Church: "I am concerned about family life in the Church. We have wonderful people, but we have too many whose families are falling apart. It is a matter of serious concern. I think it is *my most serious concern.*"[5] One of the primary reasons modern-day families are failing is anger. One of the most significant contributors to the marriage enrichment movement, Dr. David Mace, argued that if he had only one hour to help a couple do something to strengthen their marriage, he would focus on helping the couple learn to deal with anger. His rationale is that anger conceals loving and caring feelings. If one or both spouses are angry with the other, they will not allow themselves or each other to demonstrate loving and caring feelings.[6] Simply put, anger is a great destroyer of marriages and families. Elder Lynn Robbins of the First Quorum of the Seventy explained:

> [Satan] damages and often destroys families within the walls of their own homes. His strategy is to stir up anger between family members. Satan is the "father of contention, and he stirreth up the hearts of men to

contend with anger, one with another" (3 Ne. 11:29). The verb *stir* sounds like a recipe for disaster: Put tempers on medium heat, stir in a few choice words, and bring to a boil; continue stirring until thick; cool off; let feelings chill for several days; serve cold; lots of leftovers.[7]

In Satan's war on the family, he will incite, encourage, even inspire anger. But what is this anger really? Most often it is a product of Satan's old standbys of selfishness and pride. Anger results from this "me first, second, and third" mentality we have in our society. It erupts when what *we* want to have happen doesn't or when things don't go *our* way. Anger doesn't allow for humility. It boils over when our pride is hurt; it could never admit to being in the wrong. Where can we find the solutions to remedy the anger and chaos that are prevalent in too many marriages and families in the Church? Most individuals wish they knew how to control their emotions better; many wish they could do a better job of controlling their tongues. Thankfully, people can change. Old habits can be replaced with new ones.

The Great Destroyer

Anger is not a primary feeling, but a secondary emotion. It is bred by fear, frustration, hurt, and unfulfilled expectations.[8] That's right. Most people get angry when their expectations about what others should do are not met. Perhaps a father feels that his new baby should sleep all night long, especially the night before an early morning meeting. However, when the baby decides on the night before such a meeting to be cranky or sick, anger will often result. Perhaps this man will lash out at his wife in frustration because he feels that she should take care of the baby, knowing he has an important meeting the next day. Perhaps a wife will give her husband the silent treatment for several days because she has to take care of the baby every night and her husband never seems to help. This situation, and the relationship involved, deteriorates from there. We would do well to consider where our anger is really coming from and learn to confront *those* emotions. Otherwise, the anger will merely fester, and the real issue will never be resolved.

Psychologist Carlfred Broderick explained:

> The explosive expression of anger has a doubly bad effect. First it is hurtful to others and destructive of trust and intimacy. Second, it feeds upon itself within the person expressing it. That is, expressing anger breeds more anger; it does not eliminate it. . . . The Lord's position on this matter is unambiguous: there is *no* permission for losing one's temper in the circle of those who love and attempt to follow the Savior. The only righteous response to our own temper is to root it out as we would root out any other lust or excess in order to be worthy of the kingdom.[9]

Couples need to realize that it is normal to *feel* anger. In fact, there are some things you probably should get angry about, such as unfairness, injustices, inhumanity, and suffering. Some argue that anger provides individuals with the incentive to fight for humanitarian causes. Anger, some contend, is justified in cases where civil rights are violated or where the perpetrators prey upon children, the elderly, and others who need society's protection. Certainly there are cases where righteous indignation is merited, where wrongs should be righted. Even the Savior Himself became angry when His Father's house, the temple, was being desecrated. But the scriptures are clear—undisciplined anger is always, 100% of the time, cankerous, destructive, and wrong. When anger is directed toward your spouse or children, it becomes like a cancer that eats away the very foundation the relationship is built upon.

Consequences of Unchecked Anger

Not only does anger destroy relationships, but it can be transmitted through the generations, from angry parents to soon-to-be-angry children. Children's developmental years can be destroyed by anger. Elder ElRay L. Christiansen explained:

> Even in our families, situations may arise that could cause irritations. It is then that parents must be calm and exemplary.

The man with an uncontrolled temper is like an undisciplined child—he expresses his emotions explosively or by sulking, and disregards the feelings of those about him. In the home, anger should be controlled and love should abound. When, in his most impressionable years, a child experiences ugly situations that result from uncontrolled tempers, when he hears unkind words exchanged between his father and mother, and when he sees contention crowd out an atmosphere of kindness and mutual respect—when these conditions make a child's environment, what chance has he to become refined and noble? The minds of children are like the sensitive plates of a photographer; they record every incident, good and bad. Our children may forget what is said, but they never forget that which they are made to feel.[10]

Over the years that we have taught marriage and family courses and read student accounts of how parents treat their children, it seems that many do not realize that such torrential, uncontrolled, ungodly anger is a sin (see JST Eph. 4:26). There is little doubt that anger and an uncontrolled temper corrode human character—for both the giver and the recipient. In the short run, by losing our tempers, we lose the Spirit of the Lord. Without the Lord's Spirit, we will have a difficult time demonstrating charity or kindness to others. Dr. Brent Barlow gave the following caution:

One of the great inhibitors of effective communication in marriage is anger. When a husband or wife becomes angry, things are often said that cause further resentment. In addition, statements are sometimes made under the duress of anger that otherwise would not have been made. Elder Theodore M. Burton said, "Whenever you get red in the face, whenever you raise your voice, whenever you get hot under the collar, or angry, rebellious, or negative in spirit, then know that the spirit of God is leaving you and the spirit of Satan is beginning to take over."[11]

When we let contention, the spirit of Satan, take over, we are letting him win the war on our own marriage. Without the Spirit of the Lord in our lives, we cannot make it back to our Heavenly Father. The long-term penalty of uncontrolled anger could be a loss of exaltation. Therefore, there is never a good reason for outbursts of temper in family relationships. We might ask what causes such a disastrous loss of control: could it be that dinner is not ready when Dad comes home from work? Is the house a little cluttered from the play of *his* children? Maybe the sprinklers were left on too long or the thermostat was set too low or too high. Perhaps his wife was on the phone when he walked in the door. Whatever the provocation, violent, tempestuous anger is not a justified reaction. President Hinckley chastised immature husbands who fly into a rage over such trivial matters:

> No man who engages in such evil and unbecoming behavior is worthy of the priesthood of God. No man who so conducts himself is worthy of the privileges of the house of the Lord. I regret that there are some men undeserving of the love of their wives and children. There are children who fear their fathers, and wives who fear their husbands. If there be any such men within the hearing of my voice, as a servant of the Lord I rebuke you and call you to repentance. Discipline yourselves. Master your temper. Most of the things that make you angry are of very small consequence. And what a terrible price you are paying for your anger. Ask the Lord to forgive you. Ask your wife to forgive you. Apologize to your children.[12]

We are reminded of President David O. McKay's counsel that there should be no yelling unless the house is on fire.[13] When we choose to express our anger, we have lost the Lord's Spirit and, consequently, become subject to Satan's power. In Proverbs we read, "He that is slow to anger is better than the mighty" (16:32). Mighty is the man or woman who can control himself or herself, regardless of the situation. The critical issue with anger, then, is how we manage it. Experiencing feelings of anger and demonstrating anger are two different things.

Anger Is a Choice

Many professional therapists and educators believe that anger is simply a response to something adverse or negative. That is, someone cuts you off on the freeway (stimulus), and you respond by driving up next to him or her and staring them down or yelling at them. They would diagram anger this way:

Stimulus ———-> Response

The gospel model would add one more element to the anger diagram:

Stimulus ———-> Agency ———-> Response

We can *choose* not to respond in anger. In a split second, we actually have the power and the ability to make a choice as to how we will react. Therefore, if we choose to express our anger toward another, we have made a cognitive choice. For instance, this time when the spouse yells, or a motorist offends, there is a zone of sovereignty where we can decide how to act. The choices are innumerable. Instead of approaching a rude motorist, an individual could decide not to respond at all, or to wave nicely. Instead of responding negatively to a spouse's accusations, you could not respond at all, or respond quietly and meekly, or perhaps offer a hug and an apology.

Do you believe that the proper use of agency can help you control your anger? Let's look at two examples we can all relate to.

You're playing a friendly game of softball in the backyard with your family. You are the pitcher and your son is the batter. When he swings at the ball, he accidentally releases the bat, and the bat, now traveling at a high rate of speed, hits you right on the shin. After you hop around on one leg for a few minutes and eventually regain the use of your limb, you will probably say a few *chastening* words to your son or chase him around the yard, limping as you go, and yelling, "An eye for an eye!"

Now let's take the very same situation and transfer it to your ward Memorial Day picnic. You are pitching, but this time your bishop is batting. He swings at your pitch, accidentally lets go of the bat, and it hits you right in the shin. Now, how do you react? Do you stare him down? Do you take the piece of broken bat and throw it back at him? Do you say something that you'll regret the next time you go in for a temple recommend interview? Of course not. Most of us would say to our bishop, "Hey, don't worry about it. My son does stuff like this all of the time," or "Bishop, don't feel bad. Accidents happen."

Do you see the point? Anger is a choice we make given our interpretation of the circumstances. We decide how we will react in a particular setting because we do not want to make fools of ourselves in public. Christlike people, because of their understanding of the principles of the gospel, choose to respond in mature ways, no matter what the setting. They treat those who are most dear to them—their spouse and children—with at least as much consideration as they would give the general public.

Controlling Anger

Have you ever imagined what the world, or even your home, would be like if there were no outward expressions of anger? Burton Kelly has written:

> Imagine . . . a world where few . . . marriages end in divorce, few children shout at their parents, no parents abuse their children. Imagine a world of safe neighborhoods, peaceful government, and healthy citizens—largely without hypertension, headaches, or backaches. Sound like never-never land, unpeopled by mortals? Yet I have just described some of the probable effects of a world absent only one simple emotion—anger.[14]

What a wonderful world it would be if anger disappeared. If individuals could learn to control or manage their anger, we could all have peace in our homes and communities. Here are a few helpful suggestions to minimize and manage anger:

1. Understand that expressing anger is a sin. From Ephesians we read, "Can ye be angry, and not sin?" (JST Eph. 4:26). The answer to Paul's question is no. If you are expressing anger at someone else's expense, it is a sin. We further learn from the Book of Mormon that if we contend with each other, we no longer have the Spirit of the Lord with us, but, rather, the spirit of the devil. It is Satan who stirs up the hearts of men to contend and argue with each other (see 3 Ne. 11:29–30). Undisciplined anger is always cankerous and destructive.

President David O. McKay was adamant on this subject when he declared:

> You have to contribute to an ideal home by your character, controlling your passion, your temper, guarding your speech, because those things will make your home what it is and what it will radiate. . . . Never must there be expressed in a Latter-day Saint home an oath, a condemnatory term, an expression of anger or jealousy or hatred. Control it! Do not express it![15]

Make no mistake. Modern-day prophets have repeatedly counseled us to control our tongues. Instead of using our lips to destroy relationships, we can strengthen family bonds as we shower each other with positive, kind words.

2. Take responsibility for your anger and the hurt it causes. Often we will hear people say, "I just tell people how it is," as if expressing anger is a good thing, or even a gift. In reality, "telling people how it is," or openly and inappropriately expressing your anger, is not the best way to handle things. We need to realize that acting out in anger is usually dangerous. Moreover, there are some who believe that anger is something beyond their control. Many will say, "I lost my temper," or, "My husband makes me so mad." No one can *make* us mad or angry, for anger is a choice. We can choose to be angry, or we can choose not to be.[16]

3. Withdraw from the situation if you know you're going to get angry. Don't stay in the ring; get out of there quickly. Take a walk, go to another room, exercise, chop down a tree, do something else. Elder Richard L. Evans of the Quorum of the Twelve declared: "One of the safest tonics for temper is time. Many centuries ago, Seneca said, 'The best cure for anger is delay.' And the idea of counting to ten has been traced back at least as far as Thomas Jefferson, who wrote, 'When angry, count ten before you speak; if very angry, an hundred.'"[17] One of the most important reasons to withdraw is to collect your thoughts. Richard Mower has written: "The times we get angry are the times when it is hardest to think rationally and gain control; in initiating new responses that are as powerful as old habits, we must use a lot of advance preparation and creativity."[18] Again, we can make the choice ahead of time. Brigham Young said, "I charge myself not to get angry. . . . No Brigham, never let anger arise in your heart, never, never!"[19]

4. If faced with a confrontation, respond with soft answers. Often, soft answers will defuse the situation. President Hinckley has said that a healthy cornerstone to marriage is the "soft answer" and that "quiet talk is the language of love, it is the language of peace, it is the language of God."[20] President Hinckley also explained that "the voice of heaven is a still small voice; likewise, the voice of domestic peace is a quiet voice."[21]

5. Identify "trigger points." Trigger points are those cues and prompts that lead to an angry outburst. You know that the combination of spilling milk on your dress at 8:08 A.M., getting your hand slammed in the car door at 8:15 A.M., and then ramming into the trash cans with your car at 8:16 A.M. will probably lead to a loud yell or scream at 8:17 A.M. Couples need to identify those things that lead to anger and hostility. Does your partner call you a certain name, leave clothes all over the floor, and treat you rudely? What contributes to the steam that is about to blow? Understand that when certain trigger points rear their ugly heads, you should remove yourself from the situation before you regret it.

6. Use humor. Humor often diffuses tense situations. Sometimes a comment at the right time can change the feeling in the entire room. Part of humor is in keeping a proper perspective. What benefit comes from getting angry over a specific situation? Seldom does an outburst of anger change people or motivate them to do better.

7. Be proactive in controlling your anger by setting goals. Families can be a great support to those who struggle with anger issues. When one father was able to go one entire month without yelling at anyone, his wife bought him his favorite golf club. Another father was cured of his angry outbursts when he had to hand a five-dollar bill over to whichever family member he criticized. After about a week, he was both broke and cured. Learning self-mastery is a key. President David O. McKay declared: "I learned that when I was tempted to say the unkind, thoughtless thing, to put my tongue way back in my mouth and clamp my teeth down on it; and each time I did that, it was easier the next time not to say the unkind, hurtful thing."[22] Follow President McKay and set a goal to control your emotions and review that goal regularly.

8. Identify calm role models and learn from their examples. Learn from others who have gained control of their temper. Certainly there are people who live in close proximity to you who can help. Identify someone whom you can approach about this issue. If you cannot find anyone from your own family to observe (which is a possibility, because anger and criticism are traits that can be passed down through generations), take a close look at individuals from your ward and stake. Believe it or not, some of them have had to learn to control their emotions. Get suggestions from them.

9. Consider the way missionaries treat investigators. Stephen R. Covey called the process of bringing people into the Church a divine model of parenting. Consider his observation:

> People are brought into the Church when they are taught with love and testimony and the Spirit works upon them as they strive to keep their commitments. . . .
>
> This magnificent conversion model is the key to family life and marriage. We should always treat our children [and

spouse] as if they were investigators and follow the same principles that missionaries use in working with investigators. You can't force investigators; you can't ridicule and embarrass and punish them for their stupidity, their laziness, their slothfulness. You may, however, be inspired to reprove them "with sharpness when moved upon by the Holy Ghost," but you will immediately desire to reaffirm your love so that they will know there is nothing personal about it; you simply are hanging tough on divine standards and principles, and everything is geared to their happiness, growth, and development. As with missionaries and investigators, so in the home, everything is based on divine law. The ultimate end is the child's happiness and optimal growth.[23]

Can you imagine missionaries criticizing or ridiculing their investigators as they prepare them for baptism? How successful would the missionary program be if we heard a dialogue that went something like this: "You what? You didn't read your assignment last night! You little jerks. You guys never do what we ask you to do. How many times have we told you to read your assignments? At least a thousand times! My gosh, Mr. Brown, if that head of yours wasn't attached to your body, you would probably leave it at the golf course. We're going to give you one more chance, but if you blow it this time, your baptism is off." Of course, this is a ridiculous example. If missionaries treated their investigators in this manner, we would have very few converts. In reality, when missionaries deal with investigators who neglect their assignments, they usually respond by saying something like: "That's okay, Mr. and Mrs. Brown. We understand. You're really busy, so don't worry about it. Let's just try it again this week. We know that you can do it." If only we could treat our spouses and children in that same way, we would have much more happiness in our families.

10. Pray. Ask for the Lord's help. He wants you to succeed. He wants you to be able to control your anger. Said Brigham Young:

> Many men will say they have a violent temper, and try to excuse themselves for actions of which they are ashamed. I will

say, there is not a man in this house who has a more indomitable and unyielding temper than myself. But there is not a man in the world who cannot overcome his passion, if he will struggle earnestly to do so. If you find passion coming on you, go off to some place where you cannot be heard; let none of your family see you or hear you, while it is upon you, but struggle till it leaves you; and pray for strength to overcome. As I have said many times to the Elders, pray in your families; and if, when the time for prayer comes, you have not the spirit of prayer upon you, and your knees are unwilling to bow, say to them, "Knees, get down there"; make them bend, and remain there until you obtain the Spirit of the Lord. If the spirit yields to the body, it becomes corrupt; but if the body yields to the spirit it becomes pure and holy.[24]

Anger can be controlled by the Spirit. Learn to manage it. Is there anyone who would not want to be married to a saint? Is there anyone who wouldn't want to be married to someone who controls their emotions? Couples should prayerfully seek to speak to their spouses and children with "the tongue of angels" (2 Ne. 32:2). In that spirit, Brigham Young advised: "Let the father be the head of the family, the master of his own household; and let him treat them [his family] as an angel would treat them."[25]

"Let Us Oft Speak Kind Words"

There is too much contention in today's families. There are not many, even within the Church, who are living up to the charge set forth by Brigham Young to treat each other as angels. There are far too many marriages riddled with contention and discord; moreover, too many parents and children spend most of their communication time arguing and criticizing each other. Anger directed toward family members becomes a cancer that eats away at the roots of the relationship. Once the roots are destroyed, the tree falls.

If we are to have the Lord's Spirit in our homes, we must rid ourselves of anger, malice, contention, and criticism. Without divine inspiration, it is difficult to demonstrate kindness and charity; without kindness and charity expressed between family members, the family will fail. Therefore, we must be more positive and encouraging with each other. President Gordon B. Hinckley warned:

> Criticism, faultfinding, evil speaking—these are of the spirit of our day. . . . Everywhere is heard the snide remark, the sarcastic gibe, the cutting down of associates. Sadly, these are too often the essence of our conversation. In our homes, wives weep and children finally give up under the barrage of criticism leveled by husbands and fathers. Criticism is the forerunner of divorce, the cultivator of rebellion, sometimes a catalyst that leads to failure. . . . I am asking . . . that we look a little deeper for the good, that we still voices of insult and sarcasm, that we more generously compliment virtue and effort. I am not asking that all criticism be silenced. Growth comes of correction. Strength comes of repentance. Wise is the man who can acknowledge mistakes pointed out by others and change his course.

> What I am suggesting is that each of us turn from the negativism that so permeates our society and look for the remarkable good among those with whom we associate, that we speak of one another's virtues more than we speak of one another's faults, that optimism replace pessimism, that our faith exceed our fears. When I was a young man and was prone to speak critically, my father would say: "Cynics do not contribute, skeptics do not create, doubters do not achieve."[26]

Time passes too quickly for us to be enemies in our own homes. The only things that we can control are the days that still remain. With that in mind, make every day count. We need to quit tearing down, and start building up. We need to control our tongues and edify our family members.

For the natural man, anger, ridicule, and criticism come naturally. There is no talent, no restraint required in faultfinding. For spouses, it is often much easier to see the bad things our husband or wife does while ignoring the positive. On the contrary, when looking back on our own actions, we seem to remember all of the good things that we did, while conveniently forgetting the trouble we've gotten into. In mental health circles, we call this "selective neglect." Realistically, everyone makes mistakes, but we quickly forget this in pointing out the mistakes of others. Perhaps this is our pride clouding our vision again, prompting us to selfishly act out and decry the faults of our spouse. Such angry criticism will only tear us apart when we should be building.

Conclusion

We have a responsibility to make our homes and relationships into safe havens where our spouses can feel loved and secure. How is that possible? Where do we begin? Is it possible for us to change our behavior? The answer is yes, people can change. Perhaps one suggestion for change is to learn the doctrine of the taming of the tongue, as taught by James in the New Testament. In James 3:6 we read that "the tongue is a fire, a world of iniquity." This is so when we fail to bridle our tongue, as James warns earlier in the epistle (see James 1:26). Truly, our words can dictate the health of our relationships. Those spoken in critical anger can endanger a relationship beyond repair, while those offered in love can build and fortify.

President Hinckley shared the following letter from a faithful member of the Church:

> Dear President Hinckley, my husband is a righteous priesthood holder. That is the highest compliment I can pay him. When he is around it is as though the Savior himself is directing us. He is kind and gentle, always finding ways to help me and the children. He has always been the one who gets up with the children during the night. He has never raised his voice or hand to me and has been a big help during my various health problems. Although we have had our difference of opinion, we have

never had an argument and I know it is because he is so careful in the way he communicates with me. He guides us through family Book of Mormon study and prayers and has now instigated a few minutes of gospel study together in the evening after the children are in bed. He is just the best man that could ever be. I feel it is an honor to be married in the temple to such a man. We are happy and in love and life is good.[27]

Husbands, could your wives say that about you? Wouldn't it be great if they could? We can all have similar relationships. Why? Simply because anger is a choice. With the Lord's help, each of us can choose to achieve a similar ideal. It will take work, effort, sacrifice, and patience on our part. It may take a lifetime, or perhaps a little longer. But change we can, if our resolve is as deep and permanent as that of the late Apostle, Elder Charles W. Penrose, when he penned:

> School thy feelings, O my brother;
> Train thy warm, impulsive soul.
> Do not its emotions smother,
> But let wisdom's voice control.
> School thy feelings; there is power
> In the cool, collected mind.
> Passion shatters reason's tower,
> Makes the clearest vision blind.[28]

CHAPTER 8

marital intimacy

Victor L. Brown has taught, "The hunger for intimacy is, next to survival needs, our deepest human longing."[1] Perhaps the greatest joy we can have in marriage is to reveal ourselves completely to our spouses, and to "be totally accepted and loved in spite of all [our] imperfections."[2] There are several different types of intimacy in marriage: (1) emotional intimacy, which involves communication and the sharing of feelings, (2) spiritual intimacy, which entails living the gospel to the best of our abilities as a couple, always reaching for higher, righteous goals to help qualify us for eternal life, and (3) physical intimacy, which includes every aspect of a married couple's sexual relationship together, from nonsexual touching to sexual intercourse. Sharing physical intimacy assures both spouses that they are needed and loved, and, of course, such intimacy is the method by which we produce offspring.

This chapter focuses on the third aspect of intimacy, sexual relations. In the book of Genesis we read, "Therefore shall a man leave his father and his mother, and shall cleave unto his wife: and they shall be one flesh" (Gen. 2:24). This idea of "one flesh" refers to physical intimacy in marriage. This act of sexual relations is ordained of God.

This facet of the marriage relationship, though outwardly simple—the uniting of the male and female anatomy—turns out to be highly complex. There is little doubt that one of the leading causes of marital disharmony stems from misunderstandings in the sexual relationship. It was President Spencer W. Kimball who commented on marital intimacy as a factor in divorce: "If you study the divorces, as we have had to do in these past years, you will find there are one, two, three, four reasons. Generally sex is the first. They did not get along sexually. They may not say that in the court. They may not even tell their attorneys, but that is the reason."[3]

Social science research confirms what a prophet has taught. In a study several years ago, 335 divorced men and women were surveyed. Forty percent of the women and fifty-six percent of the men said that sexual problems led to their marital breakup. In fact, men ranked sexual problems as the number one cause of their divorce or separation, while women ranked lack of communication and sexual problems as the two leading causes of their breakup.[4]

"What about selfishness and pride?" you may be asking. That is, after all, what we stated earlier as the root cause of divorce. But consider the common struggles of intimacy: one partner may be demanding or withholding, selfishly denying the needs of his or her spouse. Others may, in their pride, refuse to acknowledge the problem. There is little question that the quality of a couple's sexual relationship will impact their marital satisfaction.

Unfortunately, the media has done an excellent job of contaminating our sexual culture. One can hardly walk away from any modern movie or prime-time television show without assuming that most couples are having sexual relations several times a day. And most of these passionate encounters are often between unmarried couples. Family scholar Elizabeth VanDenBerghe has written:

> [The media has] long depicted marriage as the water hose guaranteed to douse the flames of passion, perhaps within months of the ceremony. The novelists have chimed in: the philandering husband looking for excitement outside his affectionless marriage remains a staple tale. Even women in books can't seem to satisfy their physical desires within marriage. In Kate Chopin's *The Awakening*, Edna Pontellier feels so burdened by the sexual repression of her marriage she walks suicidally into the sea and drowns.[5]

Sexual relations are not automatically dulled by marriage; they can fuel the marital fire of passion or become a wedge that can drive even the sanest couples to insanity. Consider the following contrasts in how they can affect a marriage. Here are one husband's feelings about intimacy:

> For my wife and me intimacy is very much an expression of love and a renewal of our marriage covenants. We can't help but feel close to each other when we express our love for each other through such an intimate relationship that lays the foundation for our desire to serve and bless each other. Intimacy brings such pleasure and joy, as well as relaxation and it has become a major form of therapy to both of us. It is amazing how we are able to shut out the world and our troubles and focus entirely on one another at these times.

Contrast the above account with one woman's feelings:

> The problems in our marriage are serious enough that I am deathly afraid of getting pregnant. I don't want to add children to this mix, and therefore, any intimacy is dangerous. Intimacy is beginning to be such a frustrating experience that I'm losing interest rapidly.

> My husband, however, is not. He is very impatient. After just three or four days, he'll start up his sarcasm and pressure [me] to be intimate with him. As the semester ends and I become extremely busy, he seems to want it more often and more urgently. And since the only time he compliments me spontaneously is when he wants to have sex, intimacy simply doesn't hold the same attraction for me that it used to.

> Overall, intimacy has been frustrating and emotionally draining for me. I know that if/when our marriage improves, so will the intimacy. I just don't see that happening in the near future, though, and the thought of continuing to be intimate with this man is depressing and

frustrating to me. I end up feeling used, unfulfilled, and unappreciated. For now, I put it off as much as I can and give in now and then to keep him satisfied.

We hope that your feelings about intimacy would not echo those of this young wife, but we know that many marriages are in a similar condition. This need not be. It is possible for intimacy in marriage to make the relationship thrive, but only if both partners are willing to be open and honest with each other and with themselves and to sacrifice for and be sensitive to each other. This approach is where our pride and selfishness can be encountered and overcome.

The Purpose of Marital Intimacy

How should members of The Church of Jesus Christ of Latter-day Saints feel about sexual relationships in marriage? *Great!* That is our answer. We view sexual relations as an integral part of the marriage relationship. Positive sexual relations between married partners can strengthen and enhance marriage. The human desire for intimacy is God given and God ordained. Some have supposed that sexual relations between man and wife are reserved solely for the purpose of conceiving children. That is one important reason, but not the only reason.

Consider what our Church authorities have said on this subject. From Parley P. Pratt we learn:

The object of the union of the sexes is the propagation of their species, or procreation; also for mutual affection, and the cultivation of those eternal principles of never-ending charity and benevolence, which are inspired by the Eternal Spirit; also for mutual comfort and assistance in this world of toil and sorrow, and for mutual duties toward their offspring.[6]

Joseph F. Smith taught that "the lawful association of the sexes is ordained of God, not only as the sole means of race perpetuation, but for the development of higher faculties and nobler traits of human nature, which love-inspired companionship of man and woman alone can insure."[7]

Paul taught the Corinthians that "neither is the man without the woman, neither the woman without the man, in the Lord" (1 Cor. 11:11). A positive sexual relationship can bring vitality, strength, renewal, and love into a marriage and, over time, bind husbands and wives together in a weld that is stronger than death.

We understand that marriage was not designed solely for sexual activity. However, sexual intercourse fulfills a human's deepest need for intimacy. It is in this sacred union that a man and wife can demonstrate their willingness to work together and to share the joys and challenges that are unique to marriage and parenthood. Elder Jeffrey R. Holland spoke to this point when he explained:

> Such an act of love between a man and a woman is—or certainly was ordained to be—a symbol of total union: union of their hearts, their hopes, their lives, their love, their family, their future, their everything. It is a symbol that we try to suggest in the temple with a word like *seal.* The Prophet Joseph Smith once said we perhaps ought to render such a sacred bond as *welding*—that those united in matrimony and eternal families are *welded* together, inseparable if you will, to withstand the temptations of the adversary and the afflictions of mortality (see D&C 128:18).
>
> But such a total, virtually unbreakable union, such an unyielding commitment between a man and a woman, can come only with the proximity and permanence afforded in a marriage covenant, with the union of all that they possess. . . .
>
> That commandment cannot be fulfilled, and that symbolism of "one flesh" cannot be preserved, if we hastily and guiltily and surreptitiously share intimacy in a darkened corner of a darkened hour, then just as hastily and guiltily and surreptitiously retreat to our separate worlds—not to eat or live or cry or laugh together, not to do the laundry and the dishes and the homework, not to manage a budget

and pay the bills and tend the children and plan together for the future. No, we cannot do that until we are truly one—united, bound, linked, tied, welded, sealed, married.[8]

The only way to have such a poignant relationship, as Elder Holland expressed, is to share our lives together—every aspect of them. Then, and only then, will intimacy become one of the most profound experiences a married couple can share together.

Sexual relations are designed to create a physical, emotional, and spiritual union. Our Heavenly Father designed marriage, and particularly sexual relationships in marriage, so that couples who face everyday challenges will have a way to renew their relationship. Just as a good marriage increases sexual interest, healthy sexual relations add binding strength to the marriage. Sexual relations are one of the highest forms of marital therapy.

A desire to be with one's spouse sexually attests to the physical, emotional, and spiritual nourishment that every couple needs.

Contention and arguments, on the other hand, destroy feelings of love and stifle any desire to participate in such a unifying act. When our deepest feelings are ignored, our motives are impugned, or our efforts are unacknowledged and unappreciated, sexual intimacy becomes a life sentence on the rock pile. One woman reported, "Sometimes I feel like a prostitute in my own home. I have a hard time wanting to participate in any intimacy when my husband snarls and gripes about all the things that I do wrong, and then he expects me to be ready at his beck and call."

There is little doubt that physical and emotional intimacy provides security and wholesomeness to happily married couples. By giving themselves to each other, spouses convey their highest and most noble feelings of charity, love, and respect. The physical touching and stimulation of each other's bodies arouses passionate feelings unique to the couple. They have learned that they can trust their physical self to a spouse who treats them with kindness and respect.

On the other hand, nothing is more hypocritical and deceptive than the desire to use another's body for selfish gratification. No husband or wife would want to share heart and soul with someone who does not appreciate the most intimate gift we can share with each other.

Enriching Marital Intimacy

At this point, we will review some important aspects of the sexual relationship within the context of marriage. We do not claim that this list is comprehensive or all encompassing. However, these simple suggestions are a good place to start.

1. Intimacy requires the highest form of charity. Such charitable behavior is demonstrated in the forms of patience, kindness, gentleness, and, perhaps most importantly, a willingness to talk to each other about your marriage and, specifically, your sexual relationship. In a couple's intimate expressions of love, an individual's true character is revealed. That is to say that the "real" us, whether we are kind, charitable, sensitive, or selfish, will be revealed in the passionate expressions between husband and wife.

For example, some individuals, perhaps more men than women, undertake sexual relations as a form of "marital rights." Case in point: a few years ago one of the authors, Doug, was on a speaking assignment in a distant city. He was approached by a couple who had some marital difficulties. Doug asked the man to explain their marital problem. The man said, "There is not enough sex in this marriage." Doug took that to mean that his wife was an unwilling partner so sexual frequency was low. Doug then asked the man's wife for her feelings on sexual relations in marriage. Her response was unexpected: "I love it. I really enjoy marital intimacy, but not when he treats me the way he does."

Doug then asked her, in front of her husband, to give an example of what he often did to ruin their sexual relationship. She provided two examples, one dealing with his treatment of her and one indicating a lack of his parenting skills. (It is difficult for a wife to express love to her husband when he is rude, mean, and abusive to their children!) As Doug listened to her concerns, he could see they were valid. He also felt that the problems could be solved. So Doug asked the man, "Can you see what your wife is saying? It is hard for her to give herself to you when she feels like you do not respect her, when you don't romance her, and when it appears that sex must be according to your schedule." Doug assumed that the man would then have a moment of comprehension. However, the man responded, "Well, I think it is her duty," totally disregarding what she had just said. This man felt that his wife should want to be intimate with him out of a sense of duty and obligation. Well, no wonder this woman had no interest in being intimate with a husband who had such warped views on sexual intimacy. Forget the love and passion and the years together—let's just get this duty done and check the box.

This experience is similar to a counseling experience that one of the authors, Mark, had a few years ago. He was counseling with a couple, and it became very clear after a few visits that this woman no longer loved her husband. The husband was controlling, domineering, and abusive. This poor wife had hung in there for about twenty years, but she had emotionally checked out. She had no feelings whatsoever for this man who had ruined her life. He was abusive not only to her, but to the children as well. However, this woman had been so "beat down" that she couldn't even express these feelings to her husband. Mark said, "You need to tell your husband exactly how you feel. We'll do it here in the office next week, and I will help you." The wife was nervous, but she agreed.

Finally, the day arrived. The time came for this little, humble wife to face her ferocious husband. She shared with him all that he had done to her over the years—the abuse, the dominance, the selfishness—and he listened. After the wife was done spilling her beans, Mark turned to the husband and said, "So, what do you think? How do you feel about what your wife has told you?" The man agreed that he had pretty much been a jerk to his wife and had also mistreated their children. Then Mark said, "How do you feel about your wife telling you that she doesn't love you anymore and that she wants a divorce?"

The man said, "Fine."

Mark thought that this encounter had gone *too* well, so he asked, "Okay, your wife no longer loves you and wants a divorce. Do you have any questions?"

The man said yes, he did.

He then looked at his wife and said, "Can we still have sex?"

Mark then asked the man to repeat himself.

The man said, "I want to know if my wife will still have sex with me."

At this point, Mark couldn't contain himself. He said, "Wait a minute. Your wife basically hates you. You've ruined her life, and she wants a divorce. And then you have the nerve to ask, 'Can we still have sex?'"

The man responded, "Well, I need my sex."

President Spencer W. Kimball taught:

> Husband and wife . . . are authorized, in fact they are commanded, to have proper sex when they are properly married for time and eternity. That does not mean that we need to go to great extremes. That does not mean that a woman is the servant of her husband. It does not mean that any man has a right to demand sex anytime that he might want it. He should be reasonable and understanding and it should be a general program between the two, so they understand and everybody is happy about it.[9]

2. Husbands and wives must learn from each other to make their sexual relations more satisfying. Where does a husband or wife learn to be a lover or how to demonstrate love to his or her companion? From a book? A seminar? A parent? The greatest resource to help you improve your love life is your spouse. For example, appropriate touching between husband and wife should be an ongoing discussion. A wife may prefer to be touched in a certain way; in fact, some women may prefer touching and caressing to actual intercourse. The point is that a husband can't know that prior to marriage. It is important that husbands and wives help each other to learn what each one needs to enjoy their intimate exchange. One woman recently reported, "I can't stand it when my husband does _____ to me," meaning a particular sexual arousal technique. The problem was that the comment was spoken to a third party—a counselor—who really could not or would not do anything about it! Wouldn't you agree that the person who needs to hear such concerns in the husband, not the counselor?

We cannot overemphasize the point that there must be willingness on the part of both spouses to teach and learn from each other in this important aspect of marriage. Marital intimacy requires frequent monitoring by both spouses. Your best source of help and learning about passion, emotions, desires, and physical responses is the person who can make a difference and resolve the situation—your sweetheart. You two must be your own therapists in this dynamic area of marriage.

Moreover, husbands should learn early in the marriage that romance is not something that only occurs several minutes before the sex act; it should become a way of life that makes a wife feel loved and appreciated continually for her contribution to the success of the marriage. Talking together, sharing nonsexual affection, and consistent validation are helpful keys to increasing a wife's interest and enthusiasm for sexual relations. If a wife hears expressions of love only during sexual intercourse, she will no doubt be a little suspicious that her husband doesn't love her as much as he loves sex.

Marital intimacy is designed to produce a wonderful bonding process between spouses and is a new adventure for newlyweds. As Latter-day Saints, we come into marriage from a culture of abstinence. After all, how many standards nights did you attend as a youth where you were warned of the serious consequences that come from "playing with fire" and "being on the devil's turf"? Most Latter-day Saints have been taught, "No, no, no" their entire lives. Then, after a simple ceremony in the temple, it all of a sudden becomes "Yes, yes, yes." Often that transition is difficult to make and takes time and patience. The mutual task, therefore, is to help each other to an arousal of passion by providing each other with clear instructions on how you want to be loved and caressed. In this setting, husbands and wives must become exceptional teachers and eager students, for there is much to learn from each other regarding each other's roles in this sacred union. Men and women are vulnerable in this setting; consequently, feelings can be easily hurt by rude, insensitive, or inappropriate comments.

Couples need to educate themselves on how their bodies and emotions function on a sexual plane; this will provide a vocabulary with which to discuss intimacy in a way that is not hurtful to one another. Studying this subject will also help couples be more understanding concerning each other's needs and difficulties as they learn how differently their bodies respond to sexual encounters. Consider the feelings of this young woman who did not have any information prior to marriage:

> What I wish I had known about sex before I got married? How about anything! When I got married, my "little talk" with my mother consisted of her telling me that "sex is something that you just have to do when you are married." She went on to explain that my future husband had certain rights and it was my obligation to fulfill his needs. I was instructed that the best way to fill those needs was to "close your eyes and let him do what he wants, and just get it over with." Is this sound advice? I was taken to our medical doctor for a premarital exam, but nothing was said about proper procedure, techniques, or enjoyment—only the suggestion that if I didn't want to have a baby every nine months, I should go on birth-control pills.
>
> Well, with all this counsel, I got married! Probably the only good thing about those first few months was that my husband didn't get any better advice and didn't have any more experience than I did. Wow! Have we ever learned a lot! Certainly trial and error is a great way to learn, but not always the best way! That first night was a miserable experience for both of us. I did my "wifely" duty and my husband did his best to perform. It was not really enjoyable for either of us. It was a painful procedure, and I know that my husband did not enjoy hurting me. How I wish someone had told us about the magic of a lubricating gel! What a difference that would have made for us both. . . .
>
> How I wish we had been brave enough to talk to one another and try a few new things at the start of our marriage. . . . Over the years we have both gotten a little braver and a little more willing to risk sharing our likes and dislikes. Certainly, the more we have shared with one another, the more enjoyable our intimate time has become.

As we can't always rely on others to approach us with information that can apply to everyone, and because the subject is vast and cannot be addressed fully in this text, we recommend pursuing some of the additional resources available. Your gynecologist can discuss some of the technical details with you, but an LDS perspective on the subject is also important. Two LDS resources that include both scientific and gender perspectives are the books *Becoming One* by Doctors Stahman, Young, and Grover, and *Between Husband and Wife* by Stephen E. Lamb and Douglas Brinley.

3. Sexual fulfillment is closely allied with the quality of life in the nonsexual areas of marriage. Often the quality of the marriage can be gauged by what happens in the bedroom. Few husbands and wives can be angry and upset with each other and still enjoy this intimate side of marriage. Occasionally we hear someone say, "The only area where we do get along is our sex life," but that is a rare sentiment. Sexual relations are a fairly consistent barometer of how well a marriage is progressing, for if two people truly care for each other and look forward to these tender moments of touching and caressing, they already share a level of emotional acceptance and sufficient strength to tackle life's challenges.

As frequency and quality of sexual expression mirrors the marriage relationship, it is logical that for spouses to give freely and fully, there should be no fear of being hurt by a spouse who is easily irritated, harsh, sarcastic, angry, or moody. When we love and respect each other and demonstrate that love outside the bedroom, our desires to be intimate in the bedroom will most likely increase. An interesting book on this topic is entitled *Sex Begins in the Kitchen.*[10] Its theme is that both sexual desire and interest, especially for women, are closely tied to what takes place in the non-bedroom arenas. It is difficult, in other words, for a wife to give herself to a husband who is unromantic, uncharitable, or critical of her role performances but who, the moment he walks into the bedroom, shifts gears and becomes Don Juan. In order to enjoy intimate relations, a wife must feel that her husband cares about her personally and that he functions as an able companion in both marriage and parenting responsibilities.

Likewise, it is difficult for a husband to want intimate contact with a wife who is carping, critical, and emotionally insensitive. One wife shared that what really turned her mind in a sexual direction was when her husband played with their children. That act alone made her feel appreciation toward her husband, gratitude that he loved being a father, and a desire to be intimate with him. Good sexual relations are a result of a great marriage.

Though all married couples have challenges in their sexual compatibility at some time during their lives together (relations during and after pregnancy, differences about desired frequency, age and related health issues), couples who rate their marriages as satisfactory find ways to adjust to the various physical and emotional aspects of sexual relations over their life cycles. Couples who have healthy and positive sexual relationships find that they can communicate together regarding physical intimacy. Couples who can openly talk and discuss their sexual life have confidence, pleasure, self-worth, and feelings of love and appreciation.

As part of a healthy marriage, we dare say that dating and courting after the wedding may be as critical as, if not even more critical than, dating during the engagement period. Couples need to pick a "date night" and observe it almost as religiously as they do the Sabbath day. Couples need the opportunity to get away from it all and spend time together, renewing in a small way their friendship and their feelings for each other. Such courting is vital for the marriage relationship on many levels, but especially because frequent positive exchanges of ideas and feelings set the stage for heightened sexual pleasure in intimate marital contact.

4. Interest levels for sex vary. Generally, it is well known that men have a greater sexual interest. This is because orgasm (ejaculation) is more predictable and therefore probably has a greater psycho-physical connection for them. For men, sex results in climax most of the time. Women do not usually experience the same consistency. So much depends on mood, on feelings toward their husband, on physical health, and so forth. Most women do not attain orgasm every time they have sexual intercourse. In fact, some women have never experienced orgasm.

It also should be stated that there are a number of women who desire more frequent intimacy than their husband does. In fact, their overall sexual drive is higher than their husband's.

Both spouses must be sensitive to the needs of their companion's emotional, physical, and mental health. Couples can adjust to the preferred frequency of each other. For example, some couples have learned that a few quality experiences during the month far outweigh more less-quality experiences. The important issue here is that couples come to agree as to what is enjoyable, what is comfortable, and how often they should be involved with each other. It requires the attention of both to ensure that neither spouse is feeling hurt or used. Sometimes sexual intimacy can become a balancing act. Our caution here is that just because a husband may desire sex more than his wife, doesn't mean that he has the right to push his needs on a wife whose health or personal desires are temporarily off track. But both spouses should be willing to meet the needs of their sweetheart in a context of love and affection. Charity must be the overarching virtue for both spouses as mutual consideration allows each spouse to be comfortable in initiating or declining a sexual episode. Each must realize that there are times when sexual relations are not preferable, comfortable, or even desirable for their spouse.

It is also important to learn that husbands are normally sexually aroused by visual or erotic themes and messages and that wives more generally enjoy the romantic approach (flowers, a call from work, help with housework or children). Gentle and sensitive holding and touching each other, coupled with genuine expressions of love and endearment, are important elements for both spouses if they are to be faithful sweethearts.

5. *Each relationship is unique.* Both spouses need to be wise enough and sufficiently mature to realize that the only performance standards in marriage are yours; you need not compare your sexual life with what is portrayed on TV, what other couples say, or so-called "national statistics." Men are notorious for this. They want to remind their wives of some statistic that they heard while playing Trivial Pursuit—that the average couple has sexual relations two to three times a week. Such statistics, first, are questionable and, second, should not guide your love life. Who's comparing? Isn't this just

another way for pride to creep into our marriages? Your only desire should be to please each other. Find what works in your marriage and go with it. Couched in respect and love for each other, your own experiences will enrich your relationship.

Such a process takes patience, though. It usually takes some time for a couple to establish the psychological and emotional climate before this expression of loves ripens and fully blossoms. So, if you have had difficulties in this area of your marriage and you have only been married for a short while, take heart. It will get better. Be patient. Talk to each other. Work on it together. If you have been married for much longer, be patient and keep trying. You may need to see a professional sex therapist, but there is help and hope available to those who struggle in the area of physical intimacy.

Our society places so much emphasis on the frequency, technique, and skill of sexual relations that it can become easy for a couple to get distracted and lose sight of what sexual relations are all about: strengthening marriage and recommitting each other to the marriage and to family goals. Sexual relations are also the way God intended for children to be born onto this earth. If you have accomplished these purposes, you're not doing so bad, after all. Don't get caught up with the world's view of sex.

Meeting Each Other's Sexual Needs

We have seen married couples live together for years without knowing or caring how to help each other be satisfied with their sexual relationship. Sexual relations are something we learn together; it takes time and experience for us to learn to meet each other's needs. Satisfaction in the sexual arena requires a sincere desire to please each other and must be coupled with a sensitivity not to embarrass one another. It requires a sense of humor, as, for most couples, honeymoon ignorance can be quite humorous compared with what you later come to know and prefer. The point is that both spouses can help each other reach a level of sexual satisfaction and passion that can make this relationship a powerful dimension for married couples and a very important part of their lives together.

A gentle reminder here is the need to resolve any sexual problems together. Neither spouse has a problem in a vacuum. The problem of a husband troubled with premature ejaculation, for example, requires an interested and attentive wife for its resolution. If a wife cannot respond well physically, it is an issue for both spouses to address. Here are a few simple suggestions in dealing with any sexual problems:

1. Acquire a vocabulary to discuss intimacy early in marriage. It is true that most of us grow up without talking about male or female anatomy with members of the opposite sex. When we marry we are often hesitant to talk to each other until we have been married long enough to overcome our timidity and shyness.

2. Part of the charity process includes taking care of your own hygiene. Unpleasant odors can put a damper on a romantic encounter rather quickly. A shower (even together), brushing teeth, shampooing hair, and wearing deodorant, perfume, or cologne never hurts anyone. You want to be your best self in this opportunity to express your love to each other.

3. As you discover what is pleasing to you, teach or provide feedback to your spouse about it. It is your responsibility to assist your spouse in learning how to be your lover, for who else but you knows what is most stimulating and enjoyable? To obtain this information usually requires a little experience before we ourselves learn what is stimulating and enjoyable.

4. You have the responsibility to learn what constitutes a good experience for your spouse. You must learn from your sweetheart what is relaxing, stimulating, refreshing, and pleasurable. The way to teach each other how to enjoy intimate times together can be as simple as sharing these statements: "I really become aroused when you . . . ," or "How do you feel about . . . ?" or "What can I do to help you reach a level of arousal that is enjoyable for you?" or "How can I help you reach orgasm/climax more easily?"

5. For more experienced married couples, it is important to remember that a series of steps or stages exist between the first physical touch and the most passionate embrace. What have those steps been, and what are they now? These are questions that we all ought to ask ourselves periodically. It is not uncommon for couples to skip these initial steps after they have been married for a while and focus only on the final stages of sexual expression, to the detriment of one or both spouses. The greatest tenderness and romance are often expressed before or after a lovemaking episode.

Conclusion

The Lord designed intimate expressions of love and appreciation within the marriage covenant to be rewarding and fulfilling for both husband and wife. This profound sharing of the soul within the bounds of marriage is one of the highlights of married life. And it is also just one more expression *of the love that binds us eternally.* President Spencer W. Kimball explained true love this way:

> Your love, like a flower, must be nourished. There will come a great love and interdependence between you, for your love is a divine one. It is deep, inclusive, comprehensive. It is not like that association of the world which is misnamed love, but which is mostly physical attraction. When marriage is based on this only, the parties soon tire of one another. There is a break and a divorce, and a new, fresher physical attraction comes with another marriage which in turn may last only until it, too, becomes stale. The love of which the Lord speaks is not only physical attraction, but spiritual attraction as well. It is faith and confidence in, and understanding of, one another. It is a total partnership. It is companionship with common ideals and standards. It is unselfishness toward and sacrifice for one another. It is cleanliness of thought and action and faith in God and his program. It is parenthood in mortality

ever looking toward godhood and creationship, and parenthood of spirits. It is vast, all-inclusive, and limitless. This kind of love never tires or wanes. It lives on through sickness and sorrow, through prosperity and privation, through accomplishment and disappointment, through time and eternity. . . . This is the love that I feel you are bringing to one another, but even this richer, more abundant love will wilt and die if it is not given food, so you must live and treat each other in a manner that your love will grow. Today it is demonstrative love, but in the tomorrows of ten, thirty, fifty years, it will be a far greater and more intensified love, grown quieter and more dignified with the years of sacrifice, suffering, joys, and consecration to one another, to your family, and to the kingdom of God.[11]

Indeed, it is in such a relationship that personal selfishness and pride are done away, and each partner in the marriage will thrive.

CHAPTER 9

money matters

Someone said, "Before marriage, a man yearns for the woman he loves. After marriage, the 'y' becomes silent."[1] Another bright philosopher suggested, "A successful man is one who makes more money than his wife can spend. A successful woman is one who can find such a man."[2]

It is no secret that one of the major sources of marital discord is money—not that money itself is bad, but that the misuse or overuse of it is often where the trouble begins. In fact, "The American Bar Association . . . indicated that 89% of all divorces could be traced to quarrels and accusations over money."[3] "Others have estimated that 75% of all divorces result from clashes over finances. Some professional counselors indicate that four out of five families are strapped with serious money problems."[4] Another study done by the Consumer Credit Counseling Service (CCCS) revealed that 60% of married respondents reported that they often fight with their spouse over money matters, and more than 93% reported that financial problems increased the amount of stress in their lives.[5] Family scientists have documented that income and marital satisfaction are closely related. It should be noted, however, that marital satisfaction is not always the greatest when income is the highest. For most couples, marital satisfaction is dependent on a couple's feelings that their income is adequate.[6]

President Gordon B. Hinckley has observed, "I am satisfied that money is the root of more trouble in marriage than all other causes combined."[7] Without question, money *can* become the source of much conflict and strife in a marriage. Often, when we think of our common enemies in marriage—namely pride and selfishness—we think of how they translate materially. Are not issues with money nothing more than the masks our pride and selfishness hide behind? Money issues truly cause a great deal of struggle in many marriages, but it doesn't have to be this way. When couples can work through these issues as equal partners, pride and selfishness are set aside and couples have peace and unity in the home.

Uncertain Times

Several years ago, Elder Marvin J. Ashton counseled with a couple who were engaged to be married. Both had graduated from college, came from good homes, and had had rich cultural experiences. For the most part, they had prepared well for their future marriage, except for one crucial area. When Elder Ashton asked, "Who is going to manage the money in your marriage?" the future bride responded, "He is, I guess." The prospective husband then countered, "We haven't talked about that yet." Elder Ashton was shocked that this particular couple had neglected a key aspect of marital preparation—money management.[8] The response of this couple probably isn't unusual. From our collected experience, we would guess that in marriage, financial matters are often neglected or rarely discussed unless there is a problem. Then, frequently, those discussions become heated. All couples need to be proactive when it comes to money matters.

We live in times of economic uncertainty. Many of our faithful Church members are being laid off from their high-paying jobs. Many are in excessive debt. Remember the warning from President Gordon B. Hinckley:

> I am suggesting that the time has come to get our houses in order. So many of our people are living on the very edge of their incomes. In fact, some are living on borrowings.
>
> We have witnessed in recent weeks wide and fearsome swings in the markets of the world. The economy is a

fragile thing. A stumble in the economy in Jakarta or Moscow can immediately affect the entire world. It can eventually reach down to each of us as individuals. There is a portent of stormy weather ahead to which we had better give heed. . . .

But I am troubled by the huge consumer installment debt which hangs over the people of the nation, including our own people. . . .

Everyone knows that every dollar borrowed carries with it the penalty of paying interest. When money cannot be repaid, then bankruptcy follows.[9]

Will we heed a prophet's warning? Will we take this counsel? If we want to bless our marriages and our families, we will do it. Most married couples have enough to worry about. They do not need to compound these worries by contending over financial concerns. Remember President Tanner's warning: "Overindulgence and poor money management place a heavy strain on marriage relationships."[10] It takes time and effort to master healthy spending habits. Some of us may feel that there is no light at the end of the financial tunnel. If you feel that you are alone in these struggles of money matters, you're not. We all have difficulties, and there are solutions.

Discipline

Whether you have a large sum of money to manage or very little, it does not matter. The issue is never the money itself, but how you manage it. For married couples who have been employed for some time, you understand that no matter how much money you make, it is never enough. Some couples still struggle after years of marriage to make ends meet. Some can say, "When we made $10,000 a year, we barely made it; when we made $30,000 a year we barely made it; and now, as we make $70,000 a year, we are still barely making it." Why? It is a sad truth that most people spend what they make, and the more we make, the more we want. President N. Eldon Tanner explained this tendency:

> I have discovered that there is no way that you can ever earn *more* than you can spend. I am convinced that it is not the amount of money an individual earns that brings peace of mind as much as it is having *control* of his money. Money can be an obedient servant but a harsh taskmaster. Those who structure their standard of living to allow a little surplus, control their circumstances. Those who spend a little more than they earn are controlled by their circumstances. They are in bondage. . . . The key to spending less than we earn is simple—it is called discipline. Whether early in life or late, we must eventually learn to discipline ourselves, our appetites, and our economic desires. How blessed is he who learns to spend less than he earns and puts something away for a rainy day.[11]

Ah, yes—discipline. That's where the going gets tough for most folks. Janene Wolsey Baadsgaard has wisely written, "We want Hostess Cupcakes, lavish homes in the best neighborhoods, and twenty-seven pairs of designer-name athletic shoes with inflatable soles and blinking shoelaces. The problem with most wants is, once we get them, we usually want more."[12] Along the same lines, Dr. Brent Barlow contends:

> Most newlyweds should realize that more money will not solve their problems. We often assume that if we had just a few thousand dollars more each year, our financial troubles would vanish. Many are surprised to find that couples earning two hundred thousand dollars or more are sometimes among those who have the greatest money problems, simply because they haven't yet learned to manage their income. *No amount of money will suffice if husband and wife have an inadequate means of handling it.* Successful couples of lesser means are those who have learned to manage what they do have—and they are much

happier than those who have or earn vast amounts of money and yet are inept managers.[13]

So the issue, it seems, is not, "How much money?" but, "How will we manage our money?" That is where the source of the conflict lies. Some couples argue over what their money should be spent on; others disagree on how much should be saved. In one study, the question was asked, "Why is money the source of your marital quarrels?" The study showed that 49% of the couples said that money is often used in their relationship as a means to dominate or control the other partner; 34% said they fight over money because they and their spouse have different priorities when it comes to spending the money.[14] How do we align our priorities of where funds should be allocated?

Looking Ahead and Financial Priorities

Whether you failed to discuss your financial views, goals, and priorities before marriage is no longer the issue. Once married, you simply have to deal with the issues you may face. It is extremely wise to do so before marriage, and in more detail at the beginning of marriage, but there are ways to compromise and plan in unity after marriage.

Let's talk about stewardships first. "Thou shalt be diligent in preserving what thou hast, that thou mayest be a wise steward" (D&C 136:27). The Lord gave this counsel to Church members encamped at Winter Quarters in 1847, at a time when the Saints had little to preserve. How much more relevant this counsel is to us today as we try to accumulate and preserve family income and resources to carry out the Lord's work. We have a standard of living that is easily threatened by poor management, increases in the cost of living, higher taxes, a fluctuating economy, crop disasters, a sometimes fragile employment picture, and our own peculiar brand of lifestyle. Good financial practices are certainly necessary in our day to "[preserve] what thou hast."

As Latter-day Saints, we have some unique expenditures that demand we manage money well. Consider that, as faithful tithe payers, you will have to live on 90% of your income. As we have been counseled to be self-reliant, it's important to set some more of your income aside in savings as well. Moreover, as members of the Lord's Church, you may have a few more children than your neighbors, which will mean having a larger home, bigger cars, and more funds allocated for college and missions. Thinking about your financial future can prepare you for what lies ahead. If you learn the management skills required now, you'll be able to meet future, extra demands on your resources. The Savior taught, "For which of you, intending to build a tower, sitteth not down first, and counteth the cost, whether he have sufficient to finish it" (Luke 14:28). Because of all the demands placed on our incomes, we will need to prioritize and manage accordingly if we are to make it. We've got to count the costs and calculate how we will finish the course we have set.

Agreeing on financial priorities is a key to marital success. Consider the following areas:

1. Meeting current Church expenditures. When you pay tithing and fast offerings, you have a sense of well-being because you know you're pleasing Heavenly Father. Joseph Smith taught that one aspect of faith is "an actual knowledge . . . that the course of life which [we pursue] is according to the will of God."[15] Because of the promised blessing of prosperity that attends such righteousness, some young couples have the mistaken notion that paying tithing will make them rich. That isn't necessarily the case. Prosperity doesn't always mean cash flow, but "growth in the knowledge of God, and in a testimony, and in the power to live the gospel and to inspire our families to do the same. That is prosperity of the truest kind."[16] One woman couldn't understand why her family was having so many financial problems. After all, they paid their tithing faithfully. When would the windows of heaven be opened? One day, as she was watching her husband and children playing together, she realized that her family was the greatest blessing her Heavenly Father had given her. Blessings don't always come as a check in the mail. President Gordon B. Hinckley promised that if the Saints will pay their tithes and offerings, no matter how poor they are, they will always have food "in their bowls and clothing on their backs and shelter over their heads."[17] President N. Eldon Tanner further explained that prosperity from the payment of tithing may include being healthy and having a sound mind (something all parents need). He also said that prosperity includes "family solidarity and spiritual increase."[18] With such promised blessings, how can we afford *not* to pay our tithes and offerings?

2. Meeting current expenses and bills. When you undertake an obligation that requires payment, your word should be "as good as your bond." Latter-day Saints ought to be known for their honesty and work ethic; they ought to be men and women of their word. Pay your debts, and if you can't, contact the debtor and make arrangements to make payments agreeable to him and you. Elder Marvin J. Ashton said, "Latter-day Saints who ignore or avoid their creditors are entitled to feel the inner frustrations that such conduct merits, and they are not living as Latter-day Saints should!"[19]

3. Emergency funds. Short-term savings are essential to meet life's little surprises. Putting aside a little bit every paycheck will help give you some short-term savings for emergencies. Most couples do not have an emergency fund. In fact, they live so close to the financial edge—where their expenses and income are about equal—that when emergencies transpire, they are not prepared to deal with them. Babies get sick, school expenses arise, and transmissions, washing machines, and mechanical parts have a way of wearing out—and always at an inconvenient time. You might want to have what we call "tiered savings." The amounts are not the point, but to illustrate, suppose your first goal is to get several hundred dollars put aside in emergency funds. This is money that you can get your hands on fairly easily to keep operations going routinely. Another two to five hundred is in the second tier and meant for less pressing expenses, money that you would rather not touch unless there is more of a crisis. Then, maybe a thousand as a longer-range goal would be money you would hesitate to touch unless it was a true emergency. Of course, the amount depends on your individual family income and circumstances. The point is to be prepared for the unexpected, and as the Lord promised the Saints in the early days of the Church, "If ye are prepared ye shall not fear" (D&C 38:30).

4. Long-term savings. Separate from your emergency funds, long-term savings are also important. It's easy to get caught up into thinking, "We'll start to save after we pay our debts." Unfortunately, couples learn years later that getting out of debt never happened. That's strike number one. Not having any savings is strike number two. Having your daughter call from college and tell you she's getting married at Christmas is strike three. Did you know that in the United States, for every one hundred people who live to be sixty-five, only five can retire without some form of assistance from government funds or family help? Steve Albrecht has wisely written:

> You cannot be content because your lamp is full today; it may be empty tomorrow. . . . The person who consumes all of his earnings without saving for the future is like a farmer who eats his seed corn. A savings plan that is started early and added to consistently will accumulate to sizable amounts in the future. For example, if you invest an equal amount every year from age twenty-five to age sixty-five, it will grow to be worth approximately 440 times the annual investment.[20]

Plan now for your future. Any investment in this area will pay great dividends in both your financial and emotional well-being.

5. Insurance. The purpose of insurance is to preserve you against major risks that could deplete all your funds quickly. Insurance protects your most valuable assets. Such protection includes health insurance, hopefully available through your employer; life insurance; car insurance; and homeowner's or renter's insurance. These are designed to protect you against major shocks to your budget in case of a serious loss. For example, there are many newly married couples who get pregnant without having any medical insurance. If there are any complications, the costs could be astronomical. We know of a couple, and their case is not uncommon, who had to have their baby delivered by an emergency caesarean section. The hospital bill was close to twenty thousand dollars—quite a large sum for college students to deal with. Insurance is a great blessing to those who purchase it. Often monthly premiums are much cheaper than a bulk payment of twenty thousand. In today's world we can't really afford *not* to have insurance, and it should be a priority in any couple's budget. Part of providing for your family should include providing the security and stability of insurance.

6. Learn self-control. One of the most common mistakes young couples make is overspending. Often, newly married couples want to furnish their apartments with all of the gadgets that their parents had, such as computers, entertainment centers, CD players, microwave ovens, and furniture. In fact, as teachers of college-aged youth, we are always amazed at what kinds of cars we see our students driving. Some of them drive vehicles that must cost close to thirty thousand dollars. Unless parents are purchasing such vehicles for their college children, which would call for another book altogether, it would be difficult to start a marriage under such financial restraints. Elder Marvin J. Ashton taught, "Young couples should recognize that they cannot immediately maintain the same spending patterns and lifestyle as that to which they were accustomed as part of their parents' family."[21] This requires humility from both spouses. Regarding the principle of delaying gratification, Elder Joe J. Christensen shared the following experience:

> When we moved to Pullman, Washington, to attend graduate school, we had three children and Barbara was expecting our fourth. Major appliances did not come with the "temporary" World War II surplus housing apartments available for married students. . . . In a used-appliance store, we found a stove and refrigerator that cost a fraction of what we would have paid for them new. Even though we had to work with a little innovation to make the latch of the refrigerator door function, the appliances served our needs very adequately for the three years it took to finish graduate school. We then sold them to incoming married students who were delighted to pay as much as we had paid for them originally. Instead of leaving graduate school with our five children and a lot of debt, we had saved enough—through

part-time work, a fellowship, and a wife who knew how to make ends meet—to place a down payment on a big, old, modest home near the University of Idaho.[22]

One of the grand keys to avoiding financial problems is to live on less money than you earn. It is that simple.

7. Avoid debt like the plague. The lesson of living within one's means seems to be a hard one. One of the most epidemic problems in our society is that of consumer debt. In 1991, the Federal Reserve Board reported that 85% of households owed an outstanding balance on a credit card.[23] This situation has hardly improved. In a study conducted by Bae, Hanna, and Lindamood, it was reported that "40% of American households spent more than their take-home incomes and 25% of the sample spent at least 127% of their take-home income."[24] It will be difficult to maintain a successful marriage if your finances are sinking you. There is just simply too much pressure. Couples who are deep in debt spend most of their time and energy thinking and laboring over how they will get out of debt, leaving them "running on fumes" as they also must deal with other realities, such as raising their children, attending to their work responsibilities, and serving in the kingdom. It is too easy to get into debt these days. Credit card applications come in the mail at least two or three times a week. It seems that everywhere you go, whether it be an appliance store or a lumber yard, institutions are anxious to lend you money—especially at 19% to 21% interest. What this means is that if you pay only the minimum payment on your bill, it will take thirty to forty years to pay it off. That is exactly what the credit company wants. Avoid using credit cards for purchasing wants and needs. Consider the counsel provided by Elder and Sister Holland when it comes to credit cards:

> [We] encourage, if necessary, plastic surgery for both husband and wife. This is a very painless operation, and it may give you more self-esteem than a new nose job or a tummy tuck. Just cut up your credit cards. Unless you are prepared to use those cards under the strictest of conditions

and restraints, you should not use them at all—at least not at 18% or 21% or 24% interest. No convenience known to modern man has so jeopardized the financial stability of a family—especially young struggling families—as has the ubiquitous credit card.[25]

Usually, it is impossible to avoid debt when purchasing a home, a car, or education. But even with those needs, the prophets have counseled us to buy modest homes and cars. Debt, even for our needs, puts us in a tight and uncomfortable spot.

President J. Reuben Clark explained:

> [Debt] never sleeps nor sickens nor dies; . . . it works on Sundays and holidays; it never takes a vacation; . . . it has no love, no sympathy; it is as hard and soulless as a granite cliff. Once in debt, [it] is your companion every minute of the day and night; you cannot shun it or slip away from it; you cannot dismiss it; and whenever you get in its way or cross its course or fail to meet its demands, it crushes you.[26]

As we discussed before, avoid the temptation to live a lifestyle that has taken others decades to establish. Trying to maintain a lifestyle beyond your means will only cause heartache. Dr. Bernard Poduska, a professor in the Department of Family and Human Development at Brigham Young University and expert in the field of family finances, counseled:

> For the most part, debt is a symptom of trying to live beyond your means—trying to obtain status symbols that are beyond your level of income. Far too many people believe that people are worth more if they have lots of money, and are worth less if they don't. In most cases, people express their true self-worth by what they can *do*, even though they try to impress others by what they can *buy*. The need for belonging can be best satisfied through what people contribute, not through what they can consume.[27]

Part of being a wise steward is managing well the resources that you have been blessed with. Be grateful for what you have, and be prudent in your spending to avoid debt.

8. Tell your children no. For some reason, parents from every generation want their children to have more than they did. Why do we do this? Our children do not need trips to ski resorts, vacations in Europe, and a visit to the Magic Kingdom in order to be well-rounded. There are plenty of people who have never purchased Mickey Mouse ears, and they turned out just fine. As we strive to overcome our own selfish natures, we must teach the same to our children. Elder Joe J. Christensen explained:

> In our day, many children grow up with distorted values because we as parents overindulge them. Whether you are well-to-do or, like most of us, of more modest means, we as parents often attempt to provide children with almost everything they want, thus taking away from them the blessing of anticipating, of longing for something they do not have. One of the most important things we can teach our children is to deny themselves. Instant gratification generally makes for weak people. How many truly great individuals do you know who never had to struggle?

> Elder Maxwell voiced this concern when he said: "A few of our wonderful youth and young adults in the Church are unstretched. They have almost a free pass. Perks are provided, including cars complete with fuel and insurance—all paid for by parents who sometimes listen in vain for a few courteous and appreciative words. What is thus taken for granted . . . tends to underwrite selfishness and a sense of entitlement."

> And finally, in the words of Fred Gosman, "Children who always get what they want will want as long as they live." And somewhere along the line, it is important for the character development of our children to learn that "the earth still

revolves around the sun" and not around them. Rather, we should train our children to ask themselves the question, "How is the world a better place because [I am] in it?" [28]

Teach your children the value of working for what they have. The whole family will learn discipline together and will more fully appreciate the blessings in life.

9. Budgeting. President N. Eldon Tanner declared: "It has been my observation in interviewing many people through the years that far too many people do not have a workable budget and have not disciplined themselves to abide by its provisions. Many people think a budget robs them of their freedom. On the contrary, successful people have learned that a budget makes real economic freedom possible."[29]

There is no question that one of the greatest sources of prevention against debt is to live on a budget. As a married couple, you will want to have a budget to help you keep track of and organize your income and expenditures. Budgeting is an essential function for families. It is the process of anticipating income, then preplanning expenditures, and then trying to spend as you planned. Sometimes that is not always possible down to the last penny, but you ought to have an idea of what your income will be and where it needs to go to meet the financial needs of your family. Most people do not like budgeting, but many do it, whether formally or informally. Decisions have to be made anyway, so why not have a system that will allow you to monitor your expenses as you go along? Budgeting requires wisdom, self-control, goals, and a sense of direction. In order to begin a budget process, consider the following form, or create one that works for you. Notice the instructions. Go through your checkbook(s) or ledger or wherever you keep track of your expenditures, and total the actual expenditures each month for the past three months and then calculate the average monthly costs in each category. The first principle of budgeting is to see exactly where you have been allocating your funds in the past so that you can change spending directions if you need to in the coming budget period. Take a look at the categories in the sample form. You may want to customize this form and adjust it to your personal situation.

Discuss these items together, and see if you can agree on an area where your budget can be trimmed. You may want to discuss what your discretionary income goes toward.

Your Family Budget

Categories	Estimated Spending	Actual Spent
Tithing		
Donations		
Savings/Investments		
Emergency/Misc.		
Groceries		
Housing		
Utilities		
Transportation (insurance, too)		
Medical (insurance, too)		
Life Insurance		
Education		
Recreation		
Clothing		
Gifts		
Personal		
Debts*		
TOTALS		

* Debts should never exceed 20% of your net income.

For more information on this topic, we recommend that as a couple you read the following:

1. Joe J. Christensen, "Greed, Selfishness, and Overindulgence," *Ensign*, May 1999, 9–11.
2. Marvin J. Ashton, *One for the Money: Guide to Family Finance* (Salt Lake City: Intellectual Reserve, 1992; pamphlet); a booklet published by the Church and available through Church Distribution.
3. Jack M. Lyon, "How Many Loaves Have Ye?" *Ensign*, Dec. 1989, 36.

Conclusion

Even in these times of economic uncertainty, we can become disciplined and be wise stewards over what the Lord has provided for us. In this way, money issues are no longer a strain on the marriage, but an opportunity for couples to work and grow together, bonding in their efforts to provide for the family.

PART FOUR

strengths to marriage

The ultimate purpose of all we teach is to unite parents and children in faith in the Lord Jesus Christ, that they are happy at home, sealed in an eternal marriage, linked to their generations, and assured of exaltation in the presence of our Heavenly Father.

—Boyd K. Packer,
"The Shield of Faith,"
Ensign, May 1995, 8

CHAPTER 10

goals and temporal concerns

We have spent a great deal of time discussing the ways in which a marriage can struggle. It is true that there are many obstacles for married couples to deal with. But on a more positive note, there is much that married couples can do to fortify their relationships. That is where we will now shift our focus; now that we have discussed in depth the issues that can hurt a marriage, it's time to address the ones that can help it.

Goals

We'll discuss in this chapter the necessity and the wonderful opportunities of setting goals and planning together.

Unfortunately, many couples miss this chance for growth. They prepare for matrimony and marital success with even less effort than they might put into planning a family vacation. They are not prepared for the unexpected pitfalls and unforeseen situations that always lie around the next corner. Safe and successful journeys in life require planning and preparation. Likewise, successful marriages require goal setting, planning, and execution.

Our experiences with couples over the years have taught us that too few married partners have goals together. There are some who have individual goals, but it is rare to find couples who have marital goals. Most people would concur that goals are good. In fact, many believe that goal setting is related to success. It is a mystery, then, why so few people, especially couples, set goals together. Did you know that fewer than 2% of Americans set goals or have written plans for their lives? However, 95% of all successful business executives have written goals. Said Randal Wright, "Which came first—the written goal or the successful business executive? I think the answer is obvious. These men are successful because they planned to be successful and worked toward their goal. The other 98% who do not have written goals for themselves usually work for those who do."[1]

Although corporate goals are important, no one would think them more important than goals relating to the most sacred institution on the earth—marriage. In order to have a happy and thriving marriage, couples will need goals and a plan. Successful marriages just don't happen because two outstanding people are joined together in a ceremony, although some still mistakenly believe this notion. If there is one key ingredient to successful marriages, it is *work*. Such a postulation brings with it both good news and bad news. The bad news is that a successful and rewarding marriage will take effort, no matter how incredible your relationship might be.

The good news is that almost anyone can have a successful marriage if they are willing to pay the price. Yes, it may take tears and toil and commitment, but anything worthwhile always does. However, commitment alone will not be enough; couples also need direction and planning. In our clinical work, we have observed that most couples who come in for counseling often lack both commitment and direction. Most of them do not have goals together. We often take time with couples and teach them how to set goals and make plans for success in marriage. Many relationships can be rejuvenated when couples begin to set goals together. In most cases, couples know how to set goals; in fact, they may even have goals in other areas of their lives, but for some reason they have neglected to set goals in their marriage. We often find ourselves reminding couples that if goals are good for personal improvement and professional success, then they are great for strengthening marriages. President Spencer W. Kimball declared: "Goals are good. Laboring with a distant aim sets the mind in a higher key and puts us at our best. . . . We must have goals to make progress, and it's encouraged by keeping records. Progress is easier when it is timed, checked, and measured. Goals should always be made to a point that will make us reach and strain."[2]

Certainly, one of the purposes of goals is to stretch us and challenge us so that we can improve our lives and, subsequently, the lives of those around us. For example, we are aware of a husband who had a terrible temper. Although he treated his wife well, he would often take out his frustrations on his children. It wouldn't take much to set him off and have him tear into one of the children. He recognized his weakness, and he wanted to change, but he needed help. He set a goal to do a better job controlling his temper. He made a vow each week that he would not lash out at any of the children. He prayed to his Heavenly Father for help. He drew upon the powers of the Atonement. Each week in a "couple meeting," he would remind his wife of his goal. She would share with him valuable insights into his behavior and delicately point out issues that seemed to be at the root of the problem. She also did a great job of praising him for his successes and encouraging him when he failed. Eventually, he was able to get on top of his problem. Now he is working on other areas of self-improvement.

Isn't this what a marriage relationship is all about? Helping each other when we are weak? Encouraging, succoring, lifting, and healing? Decide now to be a goal-setting couple and a goal-setting family. Setting goals is very simple. A cheap date can consist of an ice-cream cone, a sheet of paper, and a pen. As you eat your ice cream, set some goals. In fact, we recommend that you set goals each month *and* review them together. Simply writing goals down won't make them work; reviewing goals is the key to success. As you review your goals together, praise each other for accomplishments and encourage each other in areas where improvement is needed.

Begin a tradition, such as designating each fast Sunday as a day to review goals with each other. Moreover, you may want to hold a weekly "couple meeting." This is just for the couple and is a time when they can meet together and talk about the calendar, their goals, the children, finances, spiritual concerns, and other family or couple issues that should be addressed without the interruption of the phone or the children.

Goals should bring us closer to the Savior and point us in the direction of the celestial kingdom. Furthermore, goals should be specific. For instance, instead of writing as a goal "become more spiritual," you should write down how you will accomplish your written goal. How are you going to become "more spiritual"? Are you going to read the scriptures more often? If so, how long are you going to read? What time of day will you begin? When will your goal be completed? Breaking goals down in this way allows them to be observed and measured. It would be hard to evaluate the progress of a generic goal like "become more spiritual." However, you can determine whether or not you read thirty minutes every day at 6:30 A.M. Therefore, goals must be specific, observable, and measurable. With each goal, make a plan of action to accompany it. We recommend that you post your written goals in a place where they can be easily seen and reviewed. You and your spouse should also frequently read and reread your patriarchal blessings and set goals based on the counsel given in them. Strive to help each other become what your Heavenly Father wants you to become. Plan time out by yourselves when you can review your goals and progress. You will see yourselves accomplish more than you thought possible in less time than you thought possible.

Positive Program of Preparation

Because some couples are not sure what areas they could focus on in goal setting, we would like to offer some suggestions. Certainly, if there is a behavior in your life that is causing your spouse pain and heartache, you may want to start there. Identify the behavior that needs to be changed, and begin to work on it.

There may be other areas of your life and aspects of your personality that need to be shored up. For instance, you may need to do better at exercising or scripture reading. You may also want to improve in your relationship with your spouse by dating each other more and arguing with each other less. These areas should all be considered "fair game" for some goal setting.

There are some other broad areas that we would like to suggest for goal setting and marital improvement. These areas include education, health, employment, financial management, and home storage. Each one of these areas can be worked on as individuals or couples.

Education

President Gordon B. Hinckley has taught: "Get all the education you can. . . . Cultivate skills of mind and hands. Education is the key to opportunity."[3] Educating our minds and spirits isn't something that ends on the day we receive our college diploma. Acquiring and applying knowledge should be a lifetime pursuit. To be on the cutting edge of your profession will certainly enhance your income and quality of life. Moreover, your education will help you acquire the talents and skills necessary to contribute to society and to the kingdom of God.

There are many opportunities outside of formal education to grow and learn. Read good books aloud to each other. Attend workshops and seminars as part of your together time. Talk to people in your ward and neighborhood and learn from them. One specific area of focus would be education in the marriage and family field.

In our counseling work, we often recommend that couples commit to spend the rest of their lives reading and learning about marriage, parenting, and other family issues. This can be done by talking about such issues with other couples, attending classes and seminars, and reading good books together. This is especially vital in this day and age. For example, years ago, couples did not need the same skills we do today to be successful as parents. In fact, such a family-friendly environment surrounded them that even parents with mediocre skills could turn out terrific kids. Schools taught values, families attended church, adults accepted their responsibilities as role models, and neighbors looked out for each other. We live in a different world today. Contemporary parents who want to be successful may be in the minority. With so little help and support from outside influences, parents most often feel alone, abandoned, and as if they were swimming upstream. Unfortunately, there is no such thing as accidental or unintentional good parenting. Today's parents must have certain skills if they are to be successful. And good parents will seek out such skills. When you finish this book, we encourage you, as a couple, to purchase a book about parenting. Read it, discuss it, set goals, and evaluate your progress.

This area of education is unlimited in its possibilities. Couples can also grow together in learning how to do home repairs, fix broken cars, plant gardens, wallpaper, paint, dance, and a myriad of other things. These areas will contribute to your self-reliance and save you money. Having such skills and knowledge will allow you to be a blessing to others as well. As a couple, consider what goals you need to set in the area of education.

Health

How many goals relating to your health did you set last New Year's Day? If you're like most Americans, you certainly considered a goal in the area of improving your physical health. We believe that being healthy is critical to a successful marriage. Dr. Victor Cline, author of *How to Make a Good Marriage Great,* explained:

> Lacking energy and good health will always affect your marriage—no matter what else about it is good and right. For one thing, it will put a damper on sex. It will also make you more vulnerable to depression. However, if your body is abounding with energy and is in top form, you will have a more positive, hopeful attitude. You will have the energy to face whatever problems and challenges confront your life together. Good health is a key factor in a sound marriage.[4]

It will be hard to have a successful marriage if couples are out of shape, have poor health, or lack the energy and stamina that it takes to maintain the intense Latter-day Saint lifestyle. We do not want to imply that couples or spouses who have poor health—and can't do anything about it—cannot be happily married. It can be done, but it is an added stress in an already stress-filled relationship. Such relationships can survive if there is a solid marital foundation in place.

For those of us who aren't doing everything we can, it is in our best interest to get into the best physical shape we possibly can. We should eat right, take vitamins, and exercise. Of course, there are many activities you can do as individuals to maintain a healthy lifestyle. However, we recommend that as a couple you also engage in physical activities together, such as jogging, tennis, or racquetball. There are plenty of physical activities that you can do that will enhance your marriage. Along these lines, marriage and family therapist Steven Braveman has contended:

> Working out together is one of the very best things a couple can do to ensure a long, vibrant and sexually satisfying relationship. Exercise stimulates the release of endorphins in the brain, giving athletes a naturally "high" sensation and greatly reducing residual body stress. It also makes a person feel more present and productive. In a relationship, this translates into less arguing, more self-confidence and more equitable balance between partners. People who exercise regularly, eat a balanced diet and drink plenty of water tend to feel empowered and naturally attractive. When both partners are actualizing this sort of lifestyle, they help draw out the best in each other and thereby increase their sense of satisfaction and attainment with the relationship.[5]

As Victor Cline noted, couples who exercise and take care of their health will have more energy; will be able to think more clearly; will be able to minimize stress, depression, and tension; and will participate in activities together that will strengthen their marriage.[6] There is certainly truth to the statement that couples who play together, stay together. We invite you to think of a physical activity that you can engage in as a couple and set some specific goals in regard to that activity. Make a plan for how you will carry out these goals.

Employment

A husband or wife's employment, or lack thereof, can certainly impact one's marriage and family relationships. Perhaps some may work in jobs that require many hours, which means being away from home much of the time. We are amazed at how many men work in different cities from where their families reside. There must be a terrible strain on a marriage when a husband and father essentially lives in another town or state. Moreover, employment stresses that impact the marriage also include overworking, traveling and being away from home, underemployment and consequent tight budgets, high-stress jobs that filter stress into the family dynamics, and unemployment.

Furthermore, in today's high-tech world, people change jobs and careers often. Young people who enter the workforce today can plan on three to four career changes and ten to twelve job changes throughout their working years.[7] So there is a need to be marketable in order to obtain the best possible job for which you are qualified. What skills can you develop that will be unique? Wives, are you prepared to work if something happens to your husbands? Husbands, what career goals do you have? How can you improve your present situation?

If you are not happy with your present employment and if it causes great stress in your marriage and family relationships, we recommend that you consider changing jobs or careers. We also suggest that you work in fields and areas that will bring you happiness and in which you can use your God-given gifts. President Howard W. Hunter counseled: "The employment we choose should be honorable and challenging. Ideally, we need to seek that work to which we are suited by interest, aptitude, and by training. A man's work should do more than provide adequate income; it should provide him with a sense of self-worth and be a pleasure—something he looks forward to each day."[8]

Set goals together in the area of employment. Find ways to improve your situation in your present job, both financially and positionally. Also, focus on goals that will make your employment better for your family; find ways to make your career lifestyle more family friendly, whether it's shortening your commute, taking more time out for your spouse and family, or whatever else you may need.

Financial Management

What are your financial goals? Do you have any? When would you like to retire? How will you pay for your children's college education?

What about missions? As discussed in the previous chapter, Latter-day Saints have many financial obligations. Having a financial plan and some goals will be very beneficial, both in the short term and long term.

As previously discussed, how a couple manages financial resources can affect the marriage relationship. Nevertheless, couples can increase their chances of having successful marriages if they can become self-reliant in several areas, finances being one of them. Elder J. Thomas Fyans maintained, "Members of the Church [are] to use their own gifts and abilities, their financial and personal resources in becoming temporally self-reliant and then reaching out to help others to gain that same capacity for self-reliance."[9] This does not mean that we all need to become millionaires, but we certainly need to be able to take care of ourselves to help build up the kingdom.

Food Storage

There are many couples who do not have goals pertaining to long-term storage of food and crucial survival supplies. However, as mentioned already, one of the keys to successful marriage is to be temporally prepared for rainy days, particularly rainy days with no food. Elder L. Tom Perry warned: "As long as I can remember, we have been taught to prepare for the future and to obtain a year's supply of necessities. I would guess that the years of plenty have almost universally caused us to set aside this counsel. I believe the time to disregard this counsel is over. With the events in the world today, it must be considered with all seriousness."[10]

Remember the words of President Ezra Taft Benson: "The revelation to produce and store food may be as essential to our temporal welfare today as boarding the ark was to the people in the days of Noah."[11] What are some goals that you could set as a couple in the area of food storage? What could you do right now to begin a home storage plan? Most wards or stakes have a calling reserved just for this area. Contact them for easy and contemporary ideas on food storage. Then set small, obtainable goals and build momentum as your resources increase.

Conclusion

Goals and dreams not written down are mere wishes. If you fail to plan for your futures, you plan to fail. The converse is also true. Remember, successful marriages are first built on the notion that you have married the "right" person. However, once married, an equally important task is to *become* the right person. Certainly, having clear-cut goals can help you become the right person.

All of us should have a plan for self-improvement. Goals should become an important part of your marriage and parenting relationships. They will assist you in leading your family to the promised land. Much like the path and the rod of iron in 1 Nephi 8, they will support you in the charge to lead your family to the Savior. If you have not made goal setting a part of your life at this point, then now is the time to begin. Find a quiet place and select some short-, medium-, and long-range goals. Doing this as a couple will not only increase your likelihood of success, but will take your marriage to a new level of vitality.

CHAPTER 11

marital communication

While attending a marriage seminar on communication, a man named Mike and his wife listened to the presenter say, "It is essential that husbands and wives know the things that are important to each other." As the presenter addressed the men in the group, he said, "Can you describe your wife's favorite flower?" Mike knew this one. He leaned over and whispered in his wife's ear, "Pillsbury All-Purpose, isn't it?"[1] This scenario illustrates the reality behind a popular bumper sticker that reads, "My wife says I don't listen to her . . . or something like that."

While one of the authors, Mark, was in college, he had a busy Saturday of studying for tests, home teaching, and doing some spring cleaning. His wife, Janie, had decided she didn't like the location of their water bed in their married-student apartment. Mark was eager to help, so, aside from some of his other activities that day, he managed to drain the water bed completely and then reset the wood frame in another part of the room. The only thing left was to fill the bladder of the bed. However, Mark also had to keep some home teaching appointments. Mark connected the water hose to the bed and turned it on. As he left the house, he yelled out to his wife, "When the bed gets full, turn the water off." What Janie heard was, "Whatever you do, don't turn the water off." When he returned two hours later, the bladder of the water bed was literally three feet above the bed frame. The bed looked like a hot-air balloon ready for takeoff. Of course, Mark's first question to Janie was, "Why in the world didn't you turn the water off?"

Her response was, "Because you said, 'Whatever you do, don't turn it off.'" What they had was the failure to *properly* communicate.

There was communication. Something is always communicated, whether you like it or not. The issue, then, and in most situations, is whether we are properly communicating.

Now, you're probably remembering how, earlier in the book, we made the claim that communication is *not* the root cause of marital discord. We stated that pride and selfishness were the culprits. So why in the *world* would we include an entire chapter on communication? Well, for several reasons. First of all, as we also stated before, communication issues do still exist as a major factor in the health of relationships. Secondly, poor communication, while not an end unto itself, can inhibit resolution of problems regarding selfishness and pride in marriage. If we can't talk about what's wrong, how can we make it right? Finally, and perhaps most important, strong communication can make any marriage stronger. As couples learn to relate better to one another, their relationship grows on a deeper level. Such bonding can really solidify a relationship, carrying it through the struggles of everyday survival to a flourishing state.

Marriage is an interesting phenomenon, when you think about it. Two people from completely different backgrounds and genders come together in a long-range commitment with little knowledge of what they will face together. Communication is the vehicle that enables couples to determine how they will deal with those challenges and to enhance and deepen their feelings for each other as they face the unknown together.

Unfortunately, for many couples, this ideal will never transpire. Sadly, we see too many couples living superficial lives together, sharing only those essential matters necessary to carry out the business side of marriage. Too few, we observe, ever get around to sharing their deepest thoughts and feelings with each other or exchanging personal dreams and ambitions. It is troubling to see couples function more like roommates, with an occasional sexual exchange, than as committed, covenant partners searching and exploring life together in a journey that includes an enriching sexual dimension. Such couples, it seems, never quite come to know the inner feelings and workings of their spouse, for they never fully engage in the profound adventure of companionship that they surely anticipated taking place before the marriage. Often, we find that such couples have friends outside the marriage who are closer to them and know them better than they know each other.

In healthy marriages, spouses share their perceptions, experiences, and feelings with each other without fear of reprisal or criticism. Communication is the medium by which such feelings and experiences are shared.

Communication Levels

We believe that there are three levels of communication specific to marriage. These levels include:

1. Superficial. This level of communication is simply a level of exchange between human beings that allows sociality, but it is not a level that builds trust and emotional closeness. It is not sufficient for married couples. Roommates maybe, but not married partners. "It's a nice day" is hardly a deep revelation that builds trust or creates much in the way of feelings. Most of us do not become emotionally involved over weather comments. Much of our daily communication with others is at this level, however, perhaps as much as eighty to ninety percent. It is a comfortable level to use anywhere because there is little risk on our part.

2. Personal. This level of communication, however, includes an exchange of topics and feelings that bring our personal opinions, ideas, values, thoughts, and the "real" us to the surface. Thus there is more risk involved with this level of communication because we are never sure how others will react when we share personally held views. This level might be illustrated with statements such as; "I think the (Republicans/Democrats) waste a lot of our money on. . . ." "The doctor thinks it may be cancer, but I'm hoping. . . ." "I don't think we should go into war unless. . . ."

This level of sharing involves more risk on our part than a superficial level does. So when we risk at this level of communication and the response of the other person is positive, we are somewhat relieved and thereby develop positive feelings that we can trust the other person because we have something in common. Human beings typically enjoy sharing personal ideas with others, and if the response is positive, a friendship begins to develop. We find someone who is like us, or thinks like we do, or at least we can communicate with them without negative responses.

At this level of risk, we do not want to be embarrassed or belittled; and in marriage we expect our personal views to be treated gently by our spouse even if we disagree. We guard against personal hurt and emotional injury. Our feelings on personal matters such as religion, politics, parenting, or philosophical positions may be such that we are hesitant to openly expose them to others if we are not sure how they will be handled by the other party; we have no past history of risk outcomes with them. This level of communication is critical for married couples because it is the way we learn about each other's views, opinions, beliefs, feelings and preferences; it is the way our feelings for each other deepen. And in marriage, we expect to come to know each other in intimate ways to a much greater extent than while dating or courting.

3. *Validation.* This level of communication is *always* positive and complimentary in tone and may be either verbal or nonverbal. "Wow, you look stunning in that outfit," or, "I have loved you since the day I first met you," would be examples of verbal expressions of validation. A wink, a glance of approval, a smile, a thumbs-up signal, or a kind touch also convey validating messages in a nonverbal way.

Typically we enjoy being around people who make us feel good and with whom we can mutually exchange ideas and compliments. On the other hand, we tend to avoid, when we can, individuals who are abrasive, condescending, or who don't think like we do. Validation strengthens a friendship. And in marriage, we want a good friend, someone with whom we share almost everything. Good friends easily share heart and soul without fear of ridicule or embarrassment. Thus, happily married couples, almost by definition, are those who find it easy to risk deeply held feelings and ideas with each other and validate each other comfortably, while couples who struggle in marriage find it difficult to be complimentary or to share their real selves for fear of being contradicted by their spouse. Their relationships become superficial because that becomes the only safe level for them to communicate at.

Intimacy is also a form of communication; the Lord designed marital intimacy to be a validating experience. Spouses who enjoy this venue of validation develop a level of trust and confidentiality that strengthens their marital bond. Obviously, the opposite is also true. When a spouse feels used or abused, intimacy is not validating, and their sexual union will not be a positive marital activity.

Human Needs

Though we have discussed extensively the different *manifestations* of human needs in men and women, all human beings have similar needs, whether they are male or female. For example, we all have a need to be loved, to feel appreciated, wanted, valued, and needed. We want to be "numero uno" to our spouse and children. We like to have our weaknesses overlooked but our strengths recognized. We have a need for touching, for intimate sharing, for friendship. We have a desire to feel included. We need our ideas to be important to others, to be creative, to feel like we are contributing in a positive way to a family or other group. Above all, we want to feel trusted. All this is played out in communication. We reach out to others and take risks in order to have these needs met and to meet these needs in others.

To illustrate the principle of risking in human interaction, let's take a common situation. Pretend for a moment that you are in a Gospel Doctrine class and that the teacher asks for comments from those in attendance. You now understand the concept of risk. You realize that if you want to say something, you do not want to embarrass yourself or the teacher. Perhaps others will think you are dumb, or maybe they will agree wholeheartedly with you, but you are not sure. You are risking a personal insight that says something about the way you think or believe. So, to avoid making yourself look less than brilliant, before you ever raise your hand to comment, you quickly rehearse in your mind what you will say. You evaluate the impact of your comment before you ever say it out loud in order to consider the reaction of those who will hear you. Much of what you do in any social situation depends on your history of making comments in public. If a teacher handles your comments well, you may be emboldened to share your ideas more often. If the stake president happens to be visiting the class that day, you may want to sit quietly and let the teacher do his or her thing, or you may make rather simple, less risky comments. But if you are comfortable with your own ideas or have confidence that you have something to contribute, you raise your hand and then actually say what you rehearsed earlier in your mind.

The point is that we risk our personal ideas according to our past experiences with risk in a particular context. This dynamic in a relationship with our spouses has even more impact on our self-esteem and our desire to communicate on nonsuperficial levels.

Integration

We need now to integrate this concept of human needs and levels of communication. As you consider the two ideas—levels of communication and human needs—what levels of communication most appropriately meet a person's needs to be loved and valued? It should be apparent that the personal and validation levels are most adept at meeting the typical needs possessed by human beings.

Perhaps we can state a principle here: if you feel worthwhile, loved, needed, and desirable, it is because you communicate with important people in your life at personal and validating levels. On the other hand, if you feel rejected, unloved, worthless, frustrated, and depressed, you are not participating in personal and validating levels of communication in your marriage, with your family or friends, or at work.

Here's the premise that we want to impress strongly upon you: it isn't that we can't or don't know how to communicate with other people; the problem is that we don't feel like risking our sense of self with someone who does not appreciate our thoughts and feelings. It is not rewarding to approach a spouse who is domineering, is overwhelming, must always be right, is easily angered, thinks that he or she came from the "true family," has answers for everything, will not discuss issues, is sarcastic, puts you down, typically disagrees with your thoughts or positions, is apathetic, or is negative with you in any other way. It is imperative that we create a safe communication environment if we are to truly take risks and share with one another.

Risk Taking

We cannot overemphasize the importance of risk-taking in marital communications. This is because if validation and the consequent sharing of personal feelings, ideas, and opinions are not taking place, it is likely that the relationship will disintegrate or reverse itself.

The net effects of negative exchanges may include a loss of confidence in one's spouse, withdrawal from each other, a return to a superficial level of communication, the withholding of personal information, mistrust of each other, anger, an increase in frustration levels, a state of "emotional divorce," and an avoidance of intimate exchanges. The marriage deteriorates to a shallower, more superficial relationship.

On the other hand, the net effect of continued risk-taking and sharing is a deeper bond. Such sharing will build trust, develop emotional closeness, strengthen love feelings, renew the relationship, make being together enjoyable, make affection natural and touching pleasurable, allow sexual intimacy to express genuine feelings of love, create a willingness to continue sharing, and help the partners become mutual therapists. In short, it will help the couple enjoy marriage. That is what every married couple should strive for. We should want to share our very souls with each other in marriage. And in a safe environment, we feel comfortable doing so.

Let us illustrate how these negative and positive exchanges function in relationships. First, a college student explains her frustration in dating a young man:

> From experience I that know the principle of risk and response is extremely important to a relationship. For over a year I dated a guy that I couldn't share anything personal with without him giving me some sarcastic remark or simply blowing the comment off. I learned pretty fast that I wasn't going to share any serious inner feelings with him. Other than that, we got along great! We could talk about superficial things all night long. We had a good time together, but there was always something missing. It took me a long time to realize that he really didn't know me or any of my dreams, ideas, or feelings. We talked about

getting married, but I knew that through the entire marriage all I could expect was superficial communication. . . . I mean, when you can't even tell someone about your favorite childhood memory or what you really want to do with your life without being ridiculed and completely ignored, then there is something wrong with that relationship, right? . . . I soon learned, however, that compromising what I needed to feel validated only made me resent my boyfriend and the whole relationship. Underneath the anger and resentment, what I really felt was hurt, because I wasn't able to share things most dear to me with a person that I wanted to know me better than anyone else.

Needless to say, this relationship didn't turn out well. I was sad, too, because I thought he was a great guy. . . . I tried asking him about his personal feelings, and all I got in response was "whatever" or "I don't care" statements. I know that he must feel deeply about some things, but I wasn't able to get him to talk about them. . . .

True to the model, it came to the point many times that it wasn't that I didn't know how to communicate or risk; it was that I absolutely did not want to share anything that would give him more ammunition to fire back at me in the form of sarcastic comments or jokes.

Imagine being in such a relationship. If you are in one now, consider how it could be if changes were made. This wife shares an experience chronicling change.

About two weeks ago Jim initiated a discussion with me. It wasn't until after our discussion in class about the importance of risk-taking that I realized that's [what had occurred]. He started by telling me how much he loved me and then asked me how I felt about our relationship. Truthfully, I had felt that we were a little distant due to [our busy lives]. He expressed that he felt something needed to change. He [felt] that . . . [we] needed to put each other first because our marriage was the most important thing in our lives. He told me he was very sorry that he hadn't been attentive lately and asked me if he had done anything to offend me. We talked about our competitive natures and a few other things. It was like a miracle. It was like he knew exactly how I was feeling. . . . I cried because it hurt my heart to know that he was so worried about us and our relationship. I was so grateful that he was so willing to tell me truthfully how he was feeling. . . .

This conversation opened my eyes! Ever since that night, something has definitely changed. We both committed to be better and to give a hundred and ten percent. Our relationship has never been bad. But this conversation took our love to a new, fresh level. He once told me, "Do you know what I want our children to remember most about me? . . . How much I love you." After this conversation I realized that he truly was trying, and I needed to be so much better. I prayed about it like I never have before and fasted about it. I found new, fun, interesting ways to tell and show him how much I loved him. I find the more I strive to love him, the more we grow closer and joy wells up in our hearts. Jim taught me a great lesson about risking. . . . Most importantly, we grew to a new, exciting level, and I know better now how to lift him and love him the way he needs me to.

When was the last time you experienced these feelings in your own marriage? Hopefully, it was not that long ago.

The Importance of Validation

Often we may forget one final point in communicating with each other. As we mentioned before, part of the reason we take risks in sharing with one another is to have our need for validation met. It is not enough to let our spouse share with us; we must take it a step further and validate the risk he or she just took in sharing with us. Who would want to live in a marriage where there is little or no validation or acknowledgment or appreciation for what we contribute to the marriage? Every spouse has a need to know that what he or she is doing has a positive effect on others. President Gordon B. Hinckley shared this story about how everyone needs validation:

> Although I should not have been, I was surprised at something President [Spencer W.] Kimball said on one occasion. I quote: "I find myself hungering and thirsting for just a word of appreciation or of honest evaluation from my superiors and my peers. I want no praise; I want no flattery; I am seeking only to know if what I gave was acceptable" (*Teachings of Spencer W. Kimball*, 489).

> If President Kimball needed a little of that, how much more do [the rest of us need it]. Perhaps I can say in this company that on one occasion I received a great shock from my mission president. I was his assistant at the time. Some of the Saints in the district had with tremendous effort put on a great program. I suggested to my mission president that we write a letter of thanks to these people for what they had done. His response was, "We do not thank people in the Church for doing their duty."

> That was the only thing I ever disagreed with him about. I believe we should thank people. I think that thanks should be genuine and sincere, as it well can be when there is honest effort and dedicated service.[2]

Validate one another. Find ways to show each other appreciation and admiration. Carefully evaluate your relationship. Does it need changing? How are we handling our stewardships in this area of validating each other?

Elder Jeffrey R. Holland gave a classic address that best illustrates this principle. Read carefully this extract:

Love is a fragile thing, and some elements in life can try to break it. Much damage can be done if we are not in tender hands, caring hands. To give ourselves totally to another person, as we do in marriage, is the most trusting step we take in any human relationship. It is a real act of faith—faith all of us must be willing to exercise. If we do it right, we end up sharing everything—all our hopes, all our fears, all our dreams, all our weaknesses, and all our joys— with another person. . . .

Sister Holland and I have been married for 37 years. . . . I may not know everything about her, but I know 39 years' worth, and she knows that much of me. . . .

The result is that I know much more clearly now how to help her, and, if I let myself, I know exactly what will hurt her. In the honesty of our love—love that can't truly be Christlike without such total devotion—surely God will hold me accountable for any pain I cause her by intentionally exploiting or hurting her when she has been so trusting of me, having long since thrown away any self-protection in order that we could be, as the scripture says, "one flesh" (Genesis 2:24). To impair or impede her in any way for my gain or vanity or emotional mastery over her should disqualify me on the spot to be her husband. . . .

In a dating and courtship relationship, I would not have you spend five minutes with someone who belittles you, who is constantly critical of you, who is cruel at your expense and may even call it humor. Life is tough enough without having the person who is supposed to love you leading the assault on your self-esteem, your sense of dignity, your confidence, and your joy. In this person's care you deserve to feel physically safe and emotionally secure. . . .

Temper tantrums are not cute even in children; they are despicable in adults, especially adults who are supposed to love each other. We are too easily provoked; we are too inclined to think that our partner meant to hurt us— meant to do us evil, so to speak; and in defensive or jealous response we too often rejoice when we see them make a mistake and find them in a fault. Let's show some discipline on this one. Act a little more maturely. Bite your tongue if you have to. "He that is slow to anger is better than the mighty; and he that ruleth his spirit than he that taketh a city" (Proverbs 16:32). At least one difference between a tolerable marriage and a great one may be that willingness in the latter to allow some things to pass without comment, without response.[3]

This last point is important. Sometimes we come home to find the sprinklers still going or the garage light on, and, as Elder Holland says, we quickly point out to our spouse that he or she is not yet ready for translation. Our suggestion, following Elder Holland's counsel, is: "Shut your big trap, turn off the light and the sprinklers, and go into the house and bless your spouse. You ain't so hot either, baby!" Remember, we are all flawed. Our role as a husband or wife is not to focus on the flaws of our partner, but to bring out their strengths. We are to *grow* together, and we can't do that without encouraging and lifting one another.

Conclusion

Be careful in how you respond to the risking and sharing of your spouse, lest you find him or her operating only at a superficial level of communication with you. Such a marriage is barely surviving. This is not what we want. Our goal should be to use communication as a tool to overcome the bad and heighten the good in a relationship. As couples, we can grow together through our communication, taking marriage to a deeper, more profound level of love.

CHAPTER 12

resolving conflicts

There are certainly many surprises in marriage. One such surprise is dealing with conflict. You were probably initially attracted to each other because of the many things you had in common (you could talk easily together, seemed to have similar values and beliefs, shared similar opinions, liked the same music, enjoyed the same foods, and so on). But now that you have been married for some time, differences in personality, character, temperament, manners, and habits have all come to the surface. You've found that there are differences where you least expected them. This is a normal part of marriage and life in general. We will all face conflict at one point or another, and no matter how mild or extreme, these conflicts can cause difficulties. Often it is in these situations when our pride truly manifests itself; we couldn't possibly be wrong, and *we* are the victims. We selfishly refuse to consider any other viewpoint. Sound familiar? This is not always how conflict has to play out in marriage, though. We can learn to accept one another's differences and still work through conflict. We can negotiate these conflicts in a caring way. Through our willingness and humility, we can overcome the difficulties of conflict, taking our marriages to a new level of vitality.

The way that couples deal with differences and conflict can make or break their marriage. Unfortunately, many couples who really never need to, end up divorcing. If there is friction in the relationship, these individuals get nervous, or at least have a brain cramp, and wonder if they should stay married. After all, they mistakenly believe, those who have successful marriages do not have conflict. This is a fallacy: every normal couple will have problems and disagreements to work through. Don't let such disagreements ruin a good relationship.

We are aware of a couple who divorced after six months of marriage. When asked why, the ex-bride said, "We just fought and argued too much. I lived in a home where my parents never had a disagreement. I didn't think couples who loved each other would argue that much." Years later, this same woman, much wiser and more mature, said, "I should never have divorced my first husband. I didn't realize until I was much older that, in fact, my parents did fight and argue; they just never did it in front of me. So I grew up thinking that if you had a good marriage, you would never contend with each other. I compared my first marriage with the fantasy of my parents' marriage, and I thought my marriage must be terrible." What a tragedy! If only this woman could have realized that disagreements and occasional spats are normal parts of marriage.

Judith Viorst has humorously described dealing with such differences:

> Before my husband and I got married, we never had fights about anything. What was there, after all, to fight about? On every fundamental issue—war, peace, race relations, religion, education, the meaning of the universe—we were in total, sweet accord. Surely we had no reason to think that this mellow state of affairs would not continue for the next forty or fifty years.
>
> From the moment we were married, we have managed to have fights about almost everything. What *isn't* there, after all, to fight about? We're still in total accord on those fundamental issues—but so what? That still leaves clothes, cooking, driving, sex, money, in-laws, children, and who gets to read the newspaper first. And there isn't the slightest possibility that this embattled state of affairs will not continue.
>
> I hadn't planned it this way. My marriage, as I too frequently informed people in my premarital innocence, was going to be a mature, intelligent relationship. If, perchance, some small disagreement happened to trouble the serenity of our days, it would be resolved promptly by rational discourse. This was a swell plan.

Unfortunately, it had nothing to do with reality. Reality, I found out in the course of our honeymoon, was my getting resentful about having to lend him my hairbrush and his getting huffy about the way I left the soap in the washbasin instead of the soap dish. Honestly, I didn't know until then that we even *had* positions on hairbrushes and soap dishes—but we do indeed. . . . We have, it turns out, passionately held positions on hundreds of subjects too lowly ever to have been thought of until we started living, day in and day out, with someone who failed to share our cherished views.[1]

Most married couples can relate well to these observations. All couples need to learn to deal with differences. One of the great myths in marriage is that disagreements, quarrels, and contention occur only in *bad* marriages. This simply is not true. Disagreements, quarrels, and contention are present in *all* marriages. In fact, our professional experience has taught us that couples who *divorce* do not have any more problems than those who *never divorce* but stay married. Put another way, couples who stay married for their lifetimes can have just as many problems as those who terminate their marriages. The main distinction between the two groups is that couples who stay married usually place a higher value on their commitment to each other and have learned to work through their problems. Elder Robert E. Wells noted:

> Whenever two people live together, they are bound to have differences of opinion. Misunderstandings can easily arise over almost every aspect of their lives—important or unimportant—such as child discipline, housekeeping, meals, money management, decorating, which radio station to play, which movie to go to, and on and on. . . .
>
> But being different doesn't necessarily mean that one person is right and the other is wrong—or that one way is better than another. Unity in marriage requires a willingness to compromise, a commitment to make the relationship

work, and a dependence on the Lord. Even though there
may be differences of opinion, habit, or background,
husbands and wives can have "their hearts knit together in
unity and in love one toward another" (Mosiah 18:21).[2]

In the early stages of marriage, we should also expect to be very
sensitive about our differences as we *learn* to work through our problems. For example, Dr. Brent Barlow shared the following experience.
After he and his wife had been married for just a few weeks, Brent's
parents telephoned one Saturday morning to indicate that they were
passing through town and would like to stop by and say hello. Brent
began to "fluff" the place up, while his new bride, Susan, began to
cook breakfast. Unknown to Brent at the time, and to most of the
male population in America, making the first meal for the in-laws is a
stressful rite of passage for new brides. So when Susan dropped the
first egg in the frying pan and the yolk broke, she instantly began to
cry. Brent was insensitive to her tears and told her to quit crying over
broken eggs. This only made matters worse. Brent didn't understand
that his new wife wanted the meal to be just right. An argument
ensued, and then the doorbell rang.

Brent and Susan went into delay mode as they warmly greeted
their family and had a good visit. However, soon after their family
departed, they were able to resume their argument almost right where
they left off. As the day wore on, three weeks' worth of past problems
surfaced. By 11:00 P.M., Brent and Susan were discussing the finer
points of their relationship, such as, "Why did we get married in the
first place?" and, "How will our marriage survive?" Remember, all of
this came about over one stupid, lousy egg.

The next day Brent and Susan found themselves in fast and testimony meeting in their new ward. They were still feeling somewhat
depressed from the night before and were wondering if their marriage
had a chance. During the meeting, an older gentleman bore his testimony. He let everyone in the congregation know that he and his wife
had been married over fifty years and had never had an argument or
expressed a cross word to each other. This only drove the Barlows into
deeper despair. Here was a man saying that he and his wife hadn't had
a disagreement in fifty years, and Brent and Susan couldn't even make

it three weeks. They left the church feeling more depressed and dejected than when they arrived.

Later that afternoon, Brent phoned his sister, who had been married several years. He asked her if she and her husband had ever been in an argument before. She let Brent know that of course they had arguments and disagreements. Brent then related the story of the old man in church who hadn't argued with his wife in fifty years. His sister concluded that either the old man was a liar, or he was extremely forgetful, or, if it really were true, what a dull and boring marriage he had had.

With the encouragement of his sister, Brent and Susan were able to mend their differences. He apologized for not being as sensitive as he should have been, and she admitted that crying over broken eggs may have been questionable. Thankfully, they were able to move forward and put their egg issues behind them.[3] However, there is a strong point to make here. Like many couples, the Barlows believed that those who have good marriages don't have problems or disagreements.

The doctrine of differences being good for us is clear. We learn in 2 Nephi 2:11 that there must be "opposition in all things." Why would marriage be excluded from "all things"? It's not. Opposition and conflict exist in the strongest marriages. But these marriages don't get strong by running from the conflicts. In fact, opposition is what makes a marriage strong. As in any area of life, marriage ties will only get stronger as couples deal well with opposition. Strength comes from resistance, opposition, and pressure.

We can apply this cliché: if it doesn't kill you, it will make you stronger (of course, this doesn't apply to abuse). The very nature of bringing two people together from different backgrounds and experiences, and subsequently having them live side by side for a lifetime, will cause most normal people to "crack" every now and again. One of the main objectives in coming to this earth in the first place is to experience problems and to learn how to resolve them. Otherwise, why come to earth at all? So here we are—a bunch of people with a bunch of problems. We all want to avoid conflict or have it immediately swept away when it arises, but no one is excluded from dealing with opposition. President Boyd K. Packer explained: "It was meant to be that life would be a challenge. To suffer some anxiety, some depression, some disappointment, even some failure is normal. Teach our members that if they have a good, miserable day once in a while, or several in a row, to stand steady and face them. Things will straighten out. There is great purpose in our struggle in life."[4]

Even the people we most admire, including prophets and Apostles, must deal with problems in marriage. Do you remember what happened with Joseph Smith and Emma one morning while Joseph was translating the Book of Mormon? Evidently Emma had done something that had offended Joseph. Soon after their disagreement, Joseph went upstairs to resume translating. However, he found that while he was still upset with Emma he could not translate a single syllable. So what did Joseph do? He went out into the orchard and prayed for direction. An hour later, Joseph got up off his knees, went directly into his house, and asked Emma to forgive him. Only then was he able to commence the translation of the Book of Mormon.[5]

Marriage is not easy, and adjustments will have to be made. After the glamour of the wedding and the drama of the honeymoon are over, you will have to settle into real life. President Spencer W. Kimball wisely counseled:

> One comes to realize very soon after the marriage that the spouse has weaknesses not previously revealed or discovered. The virtues which were constantly magnified during courtship now grow relatively smaller, and the weaknesses that seemed so small and insignificant during courtship now grow to sizable proportions. The hour has come for understanding hearts, for self-appraisal, and for good common sense, reasoning, and planning.[6]

Dealing with Differences

As we have discussed extensively, differences will and must exist in every marriage, and we must deal with them. Your ability to negotiate differences will determine whether your marriage will succeed or fail.

Diane Sollee further explains:

> After a few bad blow-ups, we become determined to avoid conflict at any cost. Successful couples are those who know how to discuss their differences in ways that actually strengthen their relationship and improve intimacy. Successful couples don't let their disagreements contaminate the rest of the relationship. While it's true that we don't get married to handle conflict, if a couple doesn't know how—or learn how—to fight or disagree successfully, they won't be able to do all the other things they got married to do. . . . We also need to realize that every happy, successful couple has approximately ten areas of disagreement that they will never resolve.[7]

What types of things do you need to be prepared to handle? What are some of the issues married couples struggle with? Recently the Association of Mormon Counselors and Psychotherapists reported on the most common problems facing couples entering marriage. The therapists ranked unrealistic expectations of marriage or spouse as the number one problem facing LDS couples entering marriage (71 percent of couples had a problem in this area), followed by problems with communication (69 percent), money management/finances (58 percent), decision making/problem solving (54 percent), power struggles (53 percent), and sex (50 percent).[8] Unfortunately, couples who are not prepared to resolve some of these problems end up terminating their marriages too quickly. You can salvage your marriage before the damage occurs by taking a preventative approach. Part of that prevention involves reading this book, but there are other possible solutions that we will discuss later.

Marital Expectations

As stated in the research provided above, *unrealistic expectations* could be the most salient problem facing your marriage right now. We dare say that most of the frustration that occurs in marriage is due to the expectations that one spouse has for the other or that both have for each other. We hear wives say, "I just thought my husband was going to help more around the house," or, "I expected that he would have been more helpful with the children." Husbands often lament, "I thought she would be more affectionate," or, "I had no idea that she was going to yell at the kids the way she does." Once again, most of the disagreements between couples come as a result of unfulfilled expectations.

So, does your spouse know what you expect from him or her? Have you discussed it lately? If you need some help, think of specific areas, such as socializing, recreation, money management, in-law relations, children, house, religious practices, job/career, etc. Make a date of it, and discuss each of these areas with each other. Find out what your sweetheart expects of you, and share what you expect of him or her.[9]

For example, one area that often causes concern is the house. Household concerns could imply anything from what you want your house to look like to whether or not you have a sprinkler system. We suggest that you discuss whose responsibility it is to keep the house clean. How do you divide up the duties? Who does the dishes? In *Stress and the Healthy Family,* family expert Delores Curran reports that one of the top marriage stressors in today's marriages for women is housekeeping standards. However, for men, housekeeping standards do not even make the top-ten list of marriage stressors.[10] No wonder household responsibilities cause so much contention in contemporary marriages. This is just one example of where expectations might be misunderstood and unmet. Take time to discuss and perhaps even write down the different expectations you have for one another in other areas, such as dealing with each other's families, your children, money and employment, Church activity, and so on. Remember the goals you discussed in chapter eleven? These may be a good place to start your discussion on expectations.

Communication

Another area where most couples get into trouble is communication. Since we have already devoted an entire chapter to communication, suffice it to say here that you will need to become good listeners. Show empathy. Share your feelings with each other in a calm, rational way. Don't walk around the room when your spouse is trying to talk with you—give him or her your full attention. Respond in considerate ways, even when you disagree. There is no room for anger or malice or contempt in marriage. President Ezra Taft Benson taught: "Restraint and self-control must be ruling principles in the marriage relationship. Couples must learn to bridle their tongues as well as their passions."[11] None of us has the right to say anything to each other unless it is positive and edifying. Then the Holy Spirit increases our ability to be kind, tenderhearted, and forgiving toward each other (see Eph. 4:29–32).

Aside from controlling our tongues, there is more that we can do to ensure better communication. We would like to suggest that all couples have a "preventative" couple's meeting regularly. When the time comes to discuss problems, Elder Robert E. Wells recommended the following:

1. Begin by sharing your gratitude for each other and reviewing blessings.

2. Discuss frustrations or problems. As you do so, keep in mind the words of Paul: "Let the husband render unto the wife due benevolence: and likewise also the wife unto the husband" (1 Cor. 7:3). Be kind and considerate to each other.

3. One of you could begin by asking, "What can I do to be a better husband/wife?"

4. As you share areas where your partner needs to change or improve, be humble and nonthreatening. Don't assume that you are always right and your partner is always wrong. Remember that it is not necessarily a matter of determining who is right and who is wrong, but of understanding each other. Understanding is the gateway to conflict resolution.

5. Do not bring a list of faults to such meetings. In fact, it may be good to limit your complaints to one or two.

6. If you are the one on the "hot seat," don't be defensive. Continually ask within your heart, "Lord, is it I?"

7. When your spouse offers you a suggestion, you can respond by saying, "You're right. I need to do better in that area." Then write some things down on a sheet of paper, and commit to your spouse some specific behaviors that you will work on.

8. Once you have gone through these steps, let the other partner share concerns and follow these same guidelines.[12]

Such charity and understanding in communication is key to dealing with differences. It is here that we can safely deal with the resistance we face in a way that will strengthen the relationship.

Negotiating Conflict

There really is no secret or rocket science to resolving concerns. It's just like anything else you do in this life—it takes some effort, thinking, and inspiration. The key is in being Christlike so that you can have the assistance of the Holy Ghost.

We would like to share with you a few ideas that will help. Try to remember that men tend to be more logical and may like to deal with the facts. Women, on the other hand, tend to be more emotional and usually prefer to deal with feelings that accompany the facts. The roles could be reversed, but either way it is good to cover all your bases when trying to resolve concerns through communication. Therefore, when resolving problems, try to remember to deal with both sides of the issue—the emotional side and the factual. This three-step model will help you work through some of the differences you have; it is not much different from the way missionaries are trained to resolve concerns with investigators. You'll notice that the model is divided into two parts: a step side and a skill side. The person who has the problem should focus on the steps, and the person who is "in trouble" should focus on the skills. This model can be diagrammed as follows:

Steps:	Skills:
1. Deal with Facts. • State the problem. • Don't attack the person.	• Focus on your partner and don't be defensive. • Ask "why" and "what" questions. • Restate (or mirror).
2. Deal with Feelings. • Use "I" statements and own the feelings. • Let your partner know if he or she has stated your feelings correctly.	• Listen. • Restate. • Show empathy. • Don't worry that you haven't shared your side of the story yet. • Apologize.
3. Resolve the Concern. • Brainstorm. • Ask your partner what he or she thinks would resolve the issue. • Commit to the solution.	• Brainstorm. • Ask your partner what he or she thinks would resolve the issue. • Commit to the solution.

Here is a demonstration of how the model should work. Let's take Carrie and Blake, for example. They have been married for three years. Carrie's entire family lives in Salt Lake City, while Blake's live in Washington State. Carrie's family is big, and they like to get together often. None of them has ever lived outside Utah, despite job offers from different places. Blake's family is a little more transient. They graduate from college and take jobs all over the country. Blake has brothers and sisters in Texas, California, Florida, Kansas, Utah, and Washington.

Nevertheless, one of Blake's concerns is that every single Sunday they have to spend the entire afternoon over at Carrie's parents' house, eating, playing games, and discussing the BYU linebacking corps for next season. Blake feels that visiting Carrie's parents' house is fine every now and then, but he is getting tired of this routine. He would like some time just to be with Carrie by himself. Even though Blake noticed this pattern before marriage, he thought that once he and Carrie got established, the visits to home would be less frequent. Instead, the visits have increased. Blake fears that he and Carrie will never have their own identity, be their own family, and have their own traditions. So, let's see how this model works. Blake and Carrie are driving from church to her parents' home for the traditional Sabbath activities. This is when Blake decides to bring the issue up.

Let's look first at what might happen if Carrie and Blake don't use this model to work through their problems. Consider the following dialogue:

> Blake: Carrie, I don't want to make you mad, but there is something I want to talk you about. Do you mind if we pull the car over and talk for a minute?

> Carrie: I don't mind. What are you thinking about?
> (They pull the car over, and the conversation begins.)

> Blake: Carrie, I'm just not sure if I want to continue going over to your parents' house every Sunday.

> Carrie: Why?

> Blake: Well, I just feel that there are certain things I would like to do on Sundays, and spending all day at your parents' house isn't the best way to spend our time.

> Carrie: Blake, I can't think of a better way to spend the Sabbath than with my family. Sunday is a family day. If you really love me, then you will spend Sundays with my family.

> Blake: It's like you think your family is the "only true family" on the earth. We never do anything with my family.

Carrie: What do you want to do, hop in the car and drive to Seattle to visit them? It's not my fault they live twelve hours away.

Blake: Look, your family makes me nauseated, okay?

Carrie: Well, you're making me nauseated.

As you can see, this is going nowhere fast. When couples are focused on themselves, they will never be able to resolve their differences. Tiny molehills can become mountains. President Gordon B. Hinckley addressed those mountains when he said: "We seldom get into trouble when we speak softly. It is only when we raise our voices that the sparks fly and tiny molehills become great mountains of contention."[13] Perhaps if they had not let themselves get so riled up, they could have resolved things. A key to using this model of resolving conflicts is to stay calm. Now let's see what happens when their conversation follows the model:

Step 1:

Blake: Carrie, I don't want to make you mad, but there is something I want to talk you about. Do you mind if we pull the car over and talk for a minute?

Carrie: I don't mind. What are you thinking about?
(They pull the car over, and the conversation begins.)

Blake: Carrie, I'm just not sure if I want to continue going over to your parents' house every Sunday.

Carrie: Why?

Blake: Well, I just feel that there are certain things I would like to do on Sundays, and I don't think that spending all day at your parents' house is the best way to spend our time.

Carrie: What would you like to do?

Blake: I would like to have some time to discuss our goals and progress as a couple. I would like time to read my scriptures, write in my journal, go for a walk, talk, read . . . you know, things like that.

Carrie: Okay, so you think we need to diversify our time, but it's not that you don't like my family.

Blake: That's pretty much it.
(Notice that they deal with the facts; Carrie doesn't let her agenda get in the way, she is not defensive—in fact, she assumes he is not implying anything negative about her family—and she focuses on Blake.)

Step 2:

Carrie: Blake, how does it make you feel when we spend all that time at my parents' house?

Blake: What do you mean?

Carrie: How do you feel? What are your feelings about me wanting to be at my parents' house all day on Sunday?

Blake: Well, I guess it makes me feel like I don't want to be there.

Carrie: That's not a feeling word. How does it make you *feel?* You know, like happy, sad, ashamed, glad, rejected . . . what? Give me a feeling.

Blake: I guess it makes me feel like you would rather be with your family than with me. So, in a way, I do feel rejected, or that I come second in your life.

Carrie: Now we're getting somewhere. I can relate to what you're saying from past experiences. Blake, I am sorry if I have made you feel that way. I didn't mean to. In fact, I just assumed that you loved being with my family as much as I do. You seem to be right in the middle of those BYU football discussions and playing computer games with my little brother.

Blake: Yeah, I'm not saying I don't like that. It's just . . .

Carrie: Just not every Sunday.

Blake: Right.

(Notice that Carrie helps Blake identify his feelings, because he isn't sure what they are. Once feelings are brought in, sometimes they serve as the solution. Also, notice how this feeling level is the perfect time to apologize.)

Step 3:

Carrie: So, what do you think we need to do here?

Blake: I don't know. I don't want you to feel that you can't see your family anymore. I want you to be close to them. I don't want to get in the way of that.

Carrie: Well, I guess we could quit going over altogether or not go over on Sundays.

Blake: Carrie, don't be drastic. For that matter I guess I could quit whining and just suck it up.

Carrie: How about this. What if we only went over every other Sunday?

Blake: Carrie, I told you that I don't want to take you

away from your family. They would hate me if they found out that I was the reason you quit coming over. Besides, you would be the only absent member in your family from American Fork to Payson. That's not going to work.

Carrie: Well, what do you think would work?

Blake: What if we continued going over, but instead of staying for six hours, we only stayed for two?

Carrie: Okay, I can make that compromise.
(Notice the compromise and commitments made. Sometimes only one party needs to change, and sometimes both need to compromise and make new commitments.)

There will be occasions in your lives when this model will not work. If this model doesn't work, then let your partner talk for five or so uninterrupted minutes while you just listen. When he or she is finished, you get your turn. When things really get out of hand, write each other a letter. That's not a bad thing to do regularly anyway.

Conclusion

As you learn to put your spouse first and strip yourself of your own pride, you will succeed in your marriage. You will be able to successfully resolve the conflicts that will enter into your relationship. As we close, consider the words of President Spencer W. Kimball:

It is certain that almost any good man and any good woman can have happiness and a successful marriage if both are willing to pay the price. . . .

I am convinced that almost any two good people can get along together and be reasonably happy together if both are totally cooperative, unselfish, and willing to work together. I realize that sometimes there are personality clashes which make the difficulty greater. . . . I want to tell you that there are no marriages that can ever be happy ones unless two people work at it. . . . The hard thing, when problems arise, is to swallow pride, eat humble pie, analyze the situation, accept the blame that is properly due and then grit one's teeth, clench one's fists, and develop the courage to say, "I'm sorry."[14]

Such humility and selflessness are the antidotes to any marital discord. Strive to live the level of righteousness President Kimball speaks of, and you will see your relationship thrive beyond what you could have ever imagined.

CHAPTER 13

how do I love thee?

In a well-known sonnet, Elizabeth Barrett Browning once wrote:

How do I love thee?
Let me count the ways.
I love thee to the depth and breadth and height
My soul can reach, when feeling out of sight
For the ends of Being and ideal Grace.[1]

Elder Holland pointed out that the question posed by Elizabeth Barrett Browning is not *when* I love thee or *why* I should love thee; the question is *how*.[2] How do you express love to your spouse? Does your spouse recognize when you are showing love? Has your wife told you lately how you can show her affection? Does your husband know when you are communicating love to him? As Elizabeth Barrett Browning put it, can our spouse count all (or any) of the ways that we show our love? By the way, there is an expert on this subject—your spouse. Have you asked him or her lately, "Honey, how can I do a better job of expressing my love to you?"

Speaking of love generally, there are a few universal principles that all husbands and wives should come to understand. Mormon taught about charity, the purest form of love: "And charity suffereth long, and is kind, and envieth not, and is not puffed up, seeketh not her own, is not easily provoked, thinketh no evil, and rejoiceth not in iniquity but rejoiceth in the truth, beareth all things, believeth all things, hopeth all things, endureth all things" (Moro. 7:45).

Put another way, a charitable husband bears his wife's imperfections patiently because he loves her. He doesn't spend his entire existence trying to correct her or groom her in his own image. The husband who possesses charity demonstrates kindness to his wife, as Mormon indicated, and he isn't jealous of her talents and strengths. He wants her to succeed by being her best self, using the talents that Heavenly Father has given her to bless her family and to contribute to the growth of the kingdom. Moreover, a husband with charity is not conceited; rather, he knows that his wife can teach him many things about himself, gospel principles, and marriage and family relationships. A righteous husband does not seek only his own interests and pleasures. He is cognizant that he is half of a larger whole. By being selfless, he puts the needs of his spouse before his own.

The charitable wife is one who tolerates her husband's imperfections. She realizes that he has never been married to her before and he doesn't know all the ins and outs of her brain unless she teaches him. She doesn't nag him into changing but genuinely loves him and inspires him to become his best self. The charitable wife is kind and demonstrates such kindness frequently. She is not jealous of her husband either; she does not feel that in order to receive more notice and attention she needs to tear him down or take away from his masculinity. A wife filled with charity places her husband's needs above her own. Together, such a couple understands that charity is the pure love of Christ; therefore, they strive to love each other with a sacred love that binds their minds and hearts together. Charity allows a couple to bear the challenges of mortality well, knowing that through their righteousness, all things will work together for their good.

Mormon continues: "Wherefore, my beloved brethren, if ye have not charity, ye are nothing, for charity never faileth. Wherefore, cleave unto charity, which is the greatest of all, for all things must fail—But charity is the pure love of Christ, and it endureth forever; and whoso is found possessed of it at the last day, it shall be well with him" (Moro. 7:46–47). Husbands, wives, does this "greatest of all" kind of love permeate your marriage? Are you building a marriage that will endure forever?

If we do not have charity, we have no claim to the celestial kingdom. If our spouse doesn't like living with us because of our temper or moodiness or criticism or carping, he or she may not want to be with us in the eternities. A temple marriage does not make eternal life automatic. If we fail in our marriage, that cannot be compensated for by success in *any* other area. It doesn't matter what college we attended, who we're related to, how much money we have, how perfect our children are, how big our home is, or if we have served in a high-profile position in the Church. If we don't have charity, we lose. End of discussion.

In Elder Hartman Rector Jr.'s last talk as a General Authority, he said that there are three things we need to do in order to gain eternal life. First, we must continually repent. Second, he said, we must forgive others. Third, "we must be nice. I do not believe there will be anyone in the celestial kingdom that is not nice."[3] Certainly, if we are not nice to our spouse, we will not be with them in the celestial kingdom, for they will not choose to be with us. To prevent this, we all need a little introspection to see if we are on track, to see if our spouse is pleased with the way we treat him or her. If we need to make changes, which we probably do, sooner is preferable to later.

A Universal Aspect of Christlike Love

Elder Jeffrey R. Holland suggested that there are several key aspects of charity that pertain to marriage. The one we wish to emphasize here is *kindness*. Certainly, showing kindness to a spouse is one of the most important elements of a happy marriage. Consider Elder Holland's message:

> "That best portion of a good man's life [is] his . . . kindness," said William Wordsworth (*Lines Composed a Few Miles Above Tintern Abbey* [1798], lines 33–35). There are lots of limitations in all of us that we hope our sweethearts will overlook. I suppose no one is as handsome or as beautiful as he or she wishes, or as brilliant in school or as witty in speech or as wealthy as we would like, but in a world of varied talents and fortunes that we can't always command, I think that makes even more attractive the qualities we can command—such qualities as thoughtfulness, patience, a kind word, and true delight in the accomplishment of

another. These cost us nothing, and they can mean *every-thing* to the one who receives them.

> I like Mormon and Paul's language that says one who truly loves is not "puffed up." Puffed up! Isn't that a great image? Haven't you ever been with someone who was so conceited, so full of themselves that they seemed like the Pillsbury Doughboy? Fred Allen said once that he saw such a fellow walking down Lovers' Lane holding his own hand. *True love blooms when we care more about another person than we care about ourselves.* That is Christ's great atoning example for us, and it ought to be more evident in the kindness we show, the respect we give, and the selflessness and courtesy we employ in our personal relationships.[4]

Notice what he mentioned we must overcome to develop true kindness—our "puffed-up," swollen pride. We all need to look inside ourselves and see if we are kind and charitable to our sweethearts. We need to become selfless, putting their needs before our own. But the question still remains, how do we do that? How can we know that we are meeting the "love" needs of our spouse?

Speaking a Foreign Tongue

During workshops on this topic, it is normal to ask the audience if there is anyone present who speaks a foreign language. Once two individuals who speak two totally different languages are identified, they come to the front of the room and greet each other in their different languages. After their exchange, we ask the audience if anyone understood a word of what was said. Oftentimes, we all understand a few words in a foreign tongue, so it may not all be "Greek." The next part is where it gets good. The two are then invited to briefly plan a family reunion in their different languages—two minutes, max, to iron out the details. Often, if the languages are rather obscure, most people in the audience do not understand a word of what was spoken, and the participants do not understand each other. The two participants are then asked to explain to the audience what they were talking about.

Once this is done, we like to ask the audience how this exercise applies to husbands and wives when it comes to the expression of their love. The answer inevitably arises that husbands and wives speak different languages, at least in terms of showing love. A husband may enjoy more physical touch than his wife. If so, he will find himself often giving love the way he wants to receive it—in some physical way. So he will often touch and massage his wife's back and neck, hold her hand, and so forth. This is how *he* speaks "love." The problem is that this may not be interpreted by the wife as *love*. She may prefer verbal compliments. Therefore, she will often praise and encourage her husband, because that, to her, is what love sounds like. Meanwhile, he may be sitting around hoping that his wife will just give him a hug and a kiss.

Do you see the problem? Like the pair speaking a foreign language, this couple's love arrows are totally missing their targets. Unfortunately, this problem is all too common. Because spouses do not understand the concept of each other's "love language," they speak a foreign tongue to each other, often resulting in one or both being frustrated when it comes to expressing love in the marriage.

Several years ago, a colleague of ours shared an experience that illustrates this principle. He and a few of his co-workers were talking at work. Our colleague said, "You know what is weird about my wife? Every day she sends me off to work with this megalunch. Then, when I get home each evening, the very first words from my wife's lips are, "'Hi, honey, how was your lunch?'" He was really perturbed about the situation. It seemed that his wife was obsessing over his lunch. She really didn't seem to care much about his day other than his megalunch. By the way, for those of us who were lunch-deprived, his lunch looked great. He usually had a couple of sandwiches, a nice apple, some tasty chips, cookies, pudding, and always a nice fruit pie.

At the same time, he murmured that his wife was more concerned about his lunch than their romantic life. He felt that area of the marriage was lacking and could use a little spark. Well, more like a bonfire. Anyway, as he explained this situation to a few of his close friends, a younger fellow working on his PhD in marriage and family relations said, "I know exactly what your problem is. Your wife is a task/service-oriented lover. You, on the other hand, are probably a touch-oriented lover." By now, the young colleague had everyone's attention. He further explained that the way our colleague's wife showed her love to him was through service, or doing tasks for him. As our friend thought about this, it was as if a switch was triggered. Instantly, he began to piece together how his wife would often serve him and do nice things for him. He began to realize that his wife showed her love to him by doing things for him, like making him a big lunch every day. The megalunch, to his wife, was equivalent to his wanting to spend a romantic evening together.

This phenomenon is described by Gary Chapman in his book *The Five Love Languages*. Chapman contends that there are five major love languages: (1) words of affirmation, (2) quality time, (3) gifts, (4) acts of service, and (5) physical touch.[5] It is typical for individuals to give love to their spouse the way they like to receive it. For instance, if you like to receive words of affirmation from others, that is the way you show love to your spouse. If you like physical contact, then that form of expression is most likely what you will dish out to your sweetheart. The point is that a good indicator of what love language you speak and understand is how you show love to others.

Love Language 1: Words of Affirmation

Elder Joe J. Christensen shared the following experience: "Once when my father-in-law was leaving the house after lunch to return to the field to work, my mother-in-law said, 'Albert, you get right back in here and tell me you love me.' He grinned and jokingly said, 'Elsie, when we were married, I told you I loved you, and if that ever changes, I'll let you know.'"[6]

Many people view love as encouraging words; for them, the audible expression of love is seen as affection. Verbal lovers need compliments, they need praise, they need encouragement. Mark Twain once said that he could live for two months on a good compliment.[7] A colleague of ours told us that if his wife would simply look at the front yard after he's mowed it and say, "Wow, those must be the straightest lawnmower tracks I have ever seen on a yard," he would be happy for the rest of the week.

While we may not understand only one love language, there are individuals who thrive on verbal expressions of love. Such spouses need to hear compliments, words of appreciation, praise, and encouragement—all validating forms of communication. Verbal-oriented sweethearts love to hear things like: "You look terrific in that outfit." "Thanks for a great meal." "I love the way you take your church calling seriously. You are so committed to the gospel." "You are a wonderful mom. I am so grateful that my children have you for their mother."

When verbal lovers hear such words, they are pleased and feel a sense of accomplishment and recognition. It makes their day.

In his book, Chapman tells the story about a husband and wife who were having some difficulty in their marriage. The wife came to Chapman's office and was particularly upset because she could not get her husband to paint a particular room in the house. She had nagged and complained to him for nine months about getting one of the bedrooms painted, and it seemed that there was nothing she could say that would inspire or motivate him to do it. Chapman's advice to the woman was to stop "riding his case" and to start praising him for the things that he did well around the home. His second piece of advice was "to never mention painting the bedroom again." Of course, the woman was not pleased with the advice she received. She saw no way that Chapman's plan could work. However, she had tried everything else, so she consented to try.

Therefore, when her husband cleaned the garage or took the garbage out or even paid the bills, she would compliment him for doing it. Since she did not know how to give compliments well, Chapman taught her to say something like this: "Bob, I really appreciate you paying the electric bill. I hear there are husbands who don't do that, and I want you to know how much I appreciate it."[8] Three weeks later, this woman reported that her husband had painted the room; all he needed was a wife who would praise him and express her appreciation for what he was doing.

So, if your spouse seems to speak this language, be aware of the need to compliment him or her. Inspire your spouse with kind, sincere compliments. Reassure him or her that you know he or she can tackle any task. One man shared with us this experience:

> When I was in graduate school, I was overwhelmed, to say the least. I had a wife and several children. I was serving in the Church, and I was also remodeling my house. Our life was out of control, and I felt like the world was caving in on me. My classes were so demanding, and I was competing with many people who were not married, who did not have families or homes to keep up. They devoted all of their waking hours to studies, while I still had bills to pay, church assignments, children's athletic games to coach and attend, classes to teach, and an incredible amount of schoolwork. There were many times that I just wanted to pack it all in and quit. Who needed that load, anyway? And besides, why did I need a Ph.D.? I would rationalize. But it was my wife who encouraged me. On those dark days when I felt like I was sinking in schoolwork, not understanding doctoral-level statistics, and wondering how I was going to turn in three thirty-page papers on different topics that were all due the same day, it was my wife who reassured me. She told me that I could do it. She made me feel like I was fully capable of carrying out this great work. Looking back on it now, I never would have been able to make it through that time of our life without my wife's complete support and her encouraging words.

Is this your love language? Are you dying to hear encouraging words from your spouse? Do you find yourself pointing things out to your spouse so that you can receive a compliment? When you do receive a compliment or praise from your spouse, do you feel that you are on top of the world? Do you find yourself showing affection by giving out praise and compliments to your spouse and family members? Do they understand that this is your way of saying, "I love you"? If so, perhaps you are a verbal lover.

Love Language 2: Quality Time

Many spouses want to be spoken to in "time language." Time is measured by the amount of it you give to another. It is taking a walk, going out to eat, sitting on a park bench together, sharing an ice cream cone, getting away for the weekend. Have you ever kept track of how much time you spend with your spouse each week? As members of the Church, we may have a few more children than most of our neighbors do. What this often translates into is that we spend most of our waking hours with our children and leave little room for our spouse. For a time-sensitive spouse, more time means more love. If couples put their marriage first, their children will reap great rewards. In fact, "evidence now overwhelmingly tells us that parents who want to rear happy, well-adjusted children need to concentrate first on their marriage."[9] In one study several years ago, over four hundred couples were surveyed. Of the 168 hours available to them during a week, most couples said they spent only around 8 hours a week together working on their marriage.[10] If we want our marriages to succeed, we must spend more time on them than we do trivial pursuits.

If "time" is the language of your spouse, you can be a blessing to him or her by spending more time together. Chapman explained, "When I sit on the couch with my wife and give her twenty minutes of my undivided attention and she does the same for me, we are giving each other twenty minutes of life. We will never have those twenty minutes again; we are giving our lives to each other. It is a powerful emotional communicator of love."[11]

It seems like this language of quality time is often spoken by women. They want to spend more time with their husbands. The problem is that most men believe that if they are in the same vicinity or neighborhood as their wife, they are spending quality time together. So, Dennis can be watching TV while his wife, Sue, is working on a project in the bedroom. In Dennis's mind, he and Sue have just spent the afternoon together. Not so! Quality time is giving your undivided attention solely to your spouse. You are totally focused upon them!

In this church, we have many things that compete with our couple time. Besides our jobs, we are busy with our children's activities,

Church callings, community involvement, and such. Time becomes a scarce resource. If your love language is quality time, you may become resentful toward the very things that keep your spouse away from you, such as jobs, children's activities, and even Church work.

Dr. Dee Hadley shared the following experience about the time that we spend with our spouses:

> Some time ago, a couple came to my office, anxious to put their marriage back on course. They had been married in the temple and were active in the Church. Unfortunately, like many couples, they thought that their marriage would take care of itself because the Lord had sanctioned it in the temple.
>
> The man was interested in bodybuilding, so I asked him how many hours a week he spent keeping his body in shape. "Two hours a day except for Sunday," he answered. Then I asked them both how many hours they spent each week making their marriage more rewarding. "Less than two hours a week," they said.
>
> This couple hadn't realized that marriage, like any other worthwhile activity, requires time and energy. It takes at least as much time to keep a marriage in shape as it does for a weight lifter to keep his body in shape. No one would try to run a business, build a house, or rear children on two to three hours a week. In fact, the more two people who love each other positively interact, the stronger their bond becomes.[12]

If you find your spouse being critical about the long hours you spend at work or the time you devote to your Church calling, he or she may be a quality-time lover. Here is another indicator: if you are craving to have time with your spouse, and even finding yourself willing to do things that you normally would not do just so you can have some time together, you are probably a quality-time lover. For instance, if you hate camping but find yourself loading up the car for the state park just to be with your spouse, this is your love language. If you are dying to go out to eat with your husband and the best thing he can come up with is meeting in the Playland at McDonald's and you take him up on it, you are definitely a person who speaks this language.

Complete this sentence: "I feel most loved by my husband/wife when _____."

If there is an emphasis on being together, quality time is probably your language.

Love Language 3: Gifts

One of our clients shared the following experience. He said that when he was growing up, his father never told him that he loved him. He heard the phrase "I love you" from his mother, but never from his father. He did notice, however, that at Christmastime, his father would go nuts when it came to buying presents for everyone. One day, just about a week before Christmas, he and his brother were shooting baskets out in the driveway. All of a sudden, their dad pulled up in the driveway with a huge ping-pong table strapped to the station wagon. He and his brother were very excited. Other Christmas gifts over the years included horses, nice bikes, video games (before anyone had video games), pool tables, and so forth. Several years later, when this young man was still craving for his father to express his love, his mother explained: "Your father loves you very much. He is not good at expressing love verbally, but the way he does it is with gifts." As the young man thought about his mother's comments, he realized that, compared to most people, he and his brothers and sisters received a hearty Christmas each year. In fact, this young man even overheard his father one time share with a relative that his favorite part of Christmas was watching the kids open their presents. This young man began to understand his father better and knew that he was loved; his father just showed it in a different way.

In many marriages, certain spouses love to receive gifts—that is their love language. A gift is evidence that you can actually hold in your hand and say, "Look, he was thinking of me," or, "She remembered me." There is no way to give a gift to someone unless you were thinking about them first. The actual gift itself is simply a symbol of the love and concern that others may have for you.

Obviously, not everyone is a gift-oriented lover. These visual or tangible symbols are not important to everyone. For example, have you ever noticed that some people never take off their wedding rings? At the same time, there are others who don't even know where their wedding ring is. You see, a gift-oriented lover would never take off a wedding ring because it is symbolic of a great gift, and it will be worn with great pride.[13]

This scenario perfectly describes people we know. Kristi has only taken her wedding ring off when she has given birth to their children. On the other hand, Jeff loses his wedding band at least once a month. Gifts do not mean much to Jeff; they mean a great deal to Kristi. Jeff related recently that their entire home is full of gifts and things that Kristi's family has given them over the years. And if such things break, you cannot throw them away, unless you want to visit the spirit world sooner than you'd planned. Kristi will not allow Jeff to throw away anything that was given to them by her family. Never mind the fact that most of these things do not work anymore. There is the bike with no seat or handlebars; there's the television set from 1963, complete with tinfoil and coat hanger for clearer reception; there's also the treadmill, with no more tread. It doesn't matter, Kristi says; these are gifts her family has given, and they mean something. Each gift, to her, represents her parents' kindness and thoughtful consideration.

For those of you who are like Jeff and not really into gift-giving, there is hope. You can speak your spouse's love language. If their language is receiving gifts, then you'd better quit reading and get shopping. Incidentally, this is one of the easiest languages to learn. Think of all the hints that have been dropped over the years, and now go out and spend some money—or, better yet, go make something by hand. Don't wait for a special occasion.

Not only do gift-oriented lovers enjoy physical gifts, but, like time lovers, they also love and often crave one of the greatest gifts of all—the gift of presence. In fact, physical presence in times of crisis is the most powerful gift you can give if your spouse's primary love language is receiving gifts. Your body is a symbol of your love. Remove the symbol, and the love evaporates.[14]

Consider the following story by a colleague:

> I made a huge mistake when our first daughter was born. I had been sitting in the hospital all day with my wife, and she was in no pain whatsoever. Her water was leaking, so she had to be admitted. We sat there watching TV all day. When the evening came, I asked her what she would think if I went home, changed clothes, dropped off my books, and . . . made sure we had enough guys for our intramural football game. She looked at me funny. I said, "If you're not okay with this, I won't go."
>
> She said, "No, go."
>
> I went, and she couldn't believe it. I asked the nurse on my way out the door if it was okay for me to leave. She assured me that my wife was far from delivering. So I left, had a great game, and came back to find my wife in sheer agony. She was now in heavy labor, and I wasn't there when she needed me the most. She didn't have the baby until 6:00 A.M. the next day, but that didn't matter. I've been in trouble ever since. That baby daughter is now almost sixteen. I have never made that mistake again!

This young married man just did not understand a few things, one of which was the importance and the tremendous power of presence. At that time in their relationship, his wife also did not understand that she needed to tell him "no." She was hoping he would read her mind, but, as she learned over time, most men are not good at guessing games.

Too often, many couples feel that they spend an adequate amount of time together each day. In reality, although they are together, this need for "presence," like the need for quality time, certainly isn't being fulfilled. Dr. Brent Barlow shared this experience:

I will never forget the moment I realized that there is more to "togetherness" than just being in each other's presence. Susan and I had just sat down to reevaluate our marriage. Nothing was really wrong at the time—we just wanted to improve. So we decided we would both jot down on paper a few things we could work on, and then we would share lists. I wrote down one or two ideas that were not that earthshaking, something like "listen more intently when the other is talking" and "help each other with tasks without being asked."

I noticed she was very thoughtful with her writing before she finally completed her list. Then we traded. Imagine my shock when I saw at the top of her list, "Spend more time with me." I was somewhat taken aback by her request and was a little alarmed. I thought I was spending adequate time with her. So we had a very interesting discussion about time and togetherness.

I conveyed to Susan that I thought we did spend time together, and she agreed. "But," she said, "sometimes you're not here at all when you're supposed to be. You're physically present but psychologically absent." I began to see what she was getting at, especially after she gave me two examples:

"When we go shopping I like to walk with you down the street or in the mall. But I'm often looking in a window at something, and you are over playing in the gutter or talking to someone else. And when we go to church, supposedly together, you sit on one end of the bench, I on the other, and our seven children all in between. Somehow I don't feel very close to you at the time. When we go to church, I want to sit by you. And I want you to hold my hand during the service."

I told my wife that sometimes when our family goes to church I feel like Snow White trying to monitor the seven dwarfs. I agreed to sit by her, but holding hands in church? I indicated that we were also supposed to listen to the sermons during the service. Susan suggested that if I practiced and had real concentration, perhaps I could do both at the same time. It might be difficult, but she felt I could do it. Now I struggle with my children each Sunday to see who is going to sit by their mother. In addition, I have found I can listen and hold my wife's hand simultaneously. Old dogs can, indeed, learn new tricks.[15]

Love Language 4: Acts of Service

Some individuals choose to express their love by doing things for others, particularly by serving their spouse and children. These are task-oriented lovers; they express love by completing the chore list and running errands. After all, someone has to take care of the messy rooms, unmowed lawn, and dirty windows. Spend a weekend cleaning out the garage with this lover, and you'll be amazed at how validated they are and what a hero you'll become.

Acts of service are things that you know your spouse would like you to do. You seek to please them by serving them. Such tasks include vacuuming, cleaning cars, painting rooms, weeding gardens, taking out garbage, cleaning up baby spills, changing diapers, cleaning the garage, and so on. You get the picture. The Savior's lesson of washing the disciples' feet fits this category. Chapman explains:

> Jesus Christ gave a simple but profound illustration of expressing love by an act of service when He washed the feet of His disciples. In a culture where people wore sandals and walked on dirt streets, it was customary for the servant of the household to wash the feet of guests as they arrived. Jesus, who had instructed His disciples to love one another, gave them an example of how to express that love when He took a basin and a towel and proceeded to wash their feet. After that simple expression of love, He encouraged His disciples to follow His example.[16]

A husband can, in effect, wash his wife's feet by helping with the household tasks, fixing a leaky faucet, helping with the laundry, picking up his clothes. A wife can wash her husband's feet by having the house look neat and clean when he comes home from work, by making his favorite meal for dinner, or by helping him clean the garage or wash cars.

Task- or service-oriented lovers express love in what they do for their spouse. Moreover, this is the way they wish to receive love from their spouse. Verbal compliments or physical affection do not fill the tank of a task-oriented lover. These people's spouses need to discover what their needs are and do all in their power to meet them. Often it is simple. Just listen to the things they typically might ask you to do, like chores around the house. Be willing to help, even before you're asked.

Consider the following story told by author Gary Gray:

> I was excited by an invitation to speak at a priesthood leadership meeting in which I would address the topic of serving my wife. With confidence, I outlined the main doctrinal points I knew were important, filled in supporting gospel illustrations, and crafted what I believed was a strong, gospel-oriented talk. I concentrated on the eternal aspects of marriage and family, summarizing the words of the prophets on the role of women and emphasizing the responsibility men have to assist them.
>
> I stayed after work one night to put the finishing touches on my talk and headed home with eager anticipation. Chris [his wife] has always been my "congregation of one" as I have outlined talks and ideas to her before presenting them in public. . . .
>
> "Chris, do you have a minute?" I asked as I came through the door.
>
> "Hi, honey. I'll be right there. I just need to check on dinner first," she replied from the back of the house.

As I walked into the living room and picked up the mail, I could hear her giving instructions to the children: Shannon was to help with dinner, Casey was to set the table, and Caitlin, our two-year-old, was to put her clothes on.

"Okay, what's up?" Chris asked after a quick kiss and hug.

"Well, I'm giving a talk in a few days at a priesthood leadership meeting. I want to read it to you so you can tell me what you think, and—"

"Just a minute, honey." Turning toward the kitchen, she called out to the children: "Shannon, the meat smells like it's burning. Casey, is the table set yet? Brianne, would you please check on Caitlin?"

She turned back to me. "Sorry. The kids are driving me crazy today. I've had to constantly remind them of the simplest things. What were you saying?"

I smiled and started over. "I've been asked to give this talk at—"

Just then Brianne walked in and said she couldn't find any clothes for Caitlin. Chris directed her to the laundry room and asked her to start another load of clothes. Before I could say another word, Caitlin came running into the room with several copies of music Chris had ordered for a choral festival.

"Oh, no!" Chris said as she hurried off to rescue a large box filled with about one hundred copies of the music. . . .

"Anyway, about my talk," I continued after she returned. "The subject is serving your spouse. I thought I would have you tell me how a priesthood holder can best serve his wife so that I can see how close I came in my draft. . . So tell me, what does a wife need the most?"

After brief reflection, Chris said, "A wife needs someone who's willing to help her do the things that she does for everyone else in the family. She needs an uncomplaining, good-natured helper who can keep focused on cleaning, cooking, shopping, child rearing, and organization—someone willing to do these things even if deserved recognition and praise do not always come. Do you have that in your talk?"

"Uh-oh," I said, lowering my gaze.

Warming to the subject, she continued, "This helper should also be able to anticipate the needs of family members, be willing to put personal projects on hold when the children need attention, and be able to quickly find family possessions."

"I don't have that in my talk either," I told her. But my talk did have plenty of good elements. "What about priesthood? Isn't it important to a wife that her husband hold the priesthood?"

She smiled. I had missed the mark only a little after all. Or so I thought. "Yes, it means a great deal to me. But what's important is using the priesthood, not just holding it. A priesthood holder should look for ways to use his priesthood to bless his wife. When a wife has to ask for help and service, she wonders if her husband is really aware of her needs. When a husband is sensitive to his wife's needs, emotions, and daily trials, she feels valued and appreciated."

"Thank you," I said, leaning over and kissing her. "What else can a husband do to serve his wife?"

"Just two more things," Chris said. "First, he should listen to her. She shouldn't have to compete with the television or the newspaper or other distractions. He should listen with his heart to what his eternal companion has to tell him. If we're going to spend eternity with each other, we ought to know each other's thoughts, opinions, worries, frustrations, and hopes."

I quietly put down the mail I still held in my hands.

"And second, he should simply love her. He should love her when she is impatient and frustrated after a busy day, or when she burns his dinner, or when she has trouble loving herself, or when she is four and a half months pregnant and doubts her ability to meet the needs of another child. And he should love her when she asks if they can eat out after a long day."

We went out for dinner that night and I rewrote my talk, emphasizing that service means much more than helping my wife only when she asks for my assistance. Chris reminded me that "true marriage," just as President Spencer W. Kimball said, is based on a happiness that "comes from giving, serving, sharing, sacrificing, and self-lessness" (*Marriage and Divorce,* Salt Lake City: Deseret Book Co., 1976, p. 12).[17]

It is evident that Gary is married to a task-oriented lover. He learned that he could express his love to his spouse by doing things for her. Without a doubt, she probably expressed her love to him in this way as well. As Dr. Chapman reminds us, our spouse's constructive criticisms about our behavior provide us with the clearest clues of their primary love language.[18] Listen to what your spouse indicates is important to him or her. If he or she always seems to "nag" you to get things done, perhaps this is just his or her way of expressing needs to be loved in this way.

Love Language 5: Physical Touch

Physical touch is one of the most powerful mediums for expressing marital love. Holding hands, kissing, embracing, and having sexual relations are all ways of communicating love to one's spouse. Can you imagine what marriage would be like without physical affection? Unfortunately, there are many physical-touch lovers who are not having their needs met by their spouses. One man explained it to his therapist this way:

> My wife is a gourmet cook. She spends hours in the kitchen. She makes these elaborate meals. Me? I'm a meat and potatoes man. I tell her she is wasting her time. I like simple food. She gets hurt and says I don't appreciate her. I do appreciate her. I just wish she would make it easy on herself and not spend so much time with the elaborate meals. Then we would have more time together, and she would have the energy to do some other things.[19]

First of all, we hope you can see part one of the problem here. If you can, you are making great progress. Obviously, this wife was a service-oriented lover. She showed her love for her husband by making meals for him. She loved to do it. Part two may be a little harder to detect. This man was a physical-touch-oriented lover. He wanted his wife to forget the chicken cordon bleu and head right to the bedroom. For all he cared, they could have eaten hot dogs and chips after a romantic evening spent in each other's arms.

For the physical-touch lover, a touch of the hand, a kiss on the cheek, or a back rub are all tantamount to saying, "I love you." Remember the different dialects here. Just because you like back rubs doesn't mean your spouse will. Keep in mind that we tend to give love the way we want to receive it. One client shared with Mark the following: "You know what my wife loves more than anything in the world? A foot rub. She loves her feet rubbed. I could care less about having my feet rubbed. That would be the last thing on my list. So, my wife is rubbing my feet, and I'm rubbing her back. Why am I rubbing her back? Because I guess that is what I would like her to do for me. For that same reason, she's rubbing my feet. I guess we've got our wires crossed."

The touch that brings pleasure to you will not necessarily bring pleasure to your spouse.

For the spouse who speaks the language of physical touch, they emotionally yearn for their spouse to reach out and touch them physically. Running a hand through the hair, giving a back rub, holding hands, embracing, initiating sexual relations—all of these and more are the emotional lifelines for this love language.

Now, we would like to give some special counsel to the men here. Most men, by nature, feel that they are touch-oriented lovers because they pursue sexual intimacy more than their wives. However, consider this question. Let's say that you are watching your favorite football team play on television, or, better yet, you are painting your living room. Now, your wife comes up to you and begins to rub your back or your head, or begins to kiss you on the cheek or nibble on your ear. What are you doing now? What is your reaction to all of this? Do you really enjoy your wife running her hand through your hair or giving you a back rub or holding hands or kissing you when you're not being intimate?

If you are a true touch-oriented lover, you will immediately turn the game off or put the paint away for another day. That's the end of that story. However, a good indicator that physical touch is not your primary love language would be if you were not interested in such affection or expressions of love. For instance, if you said something like, "That's nice, honey, but can't you see I'm trying to watch the game?" or, "Honey, please, I'm trying to focus on painting here, and you're messing me up," the chances are good that you are not a touch-oriented lover.

Discovering and Speaking Your Spouse's Primary Love Language

By now you have probably discovered your primary love language. You have read a little bit about each language and perhaps said, "That sounds just like me." Maybe a few of you are multilingual, as you seem to be characterized by more than one love language.

Even if you think that you may speak several love languages, you will be dominant in one. If you still are not sure what language you speak, we recommend that you read *The Five Love Languages* by Gary Chapman, or you may want to visit Chapman's Web site.

Take time now to tell each other what your primary love language is. If you are still not sure, try your best to answer the following questions:

1. What makes you feel most loved by your spouse? What do you desire above all else?

2. What does your spouse do or say that hurts you deeply? If, for example, your deepest pain is the critical, judgmental words of your spouse, then you may be a verbal lover. The opposite of what hurts you most is probably your love language.

3. What have you most often requested of your spouse? (The thing you have most often requested is likely the thing that would make you feel most loved.)

4. In what way do you regularly express love to your spouse? Your method of expressing love may be an indication of what would also make you feel loved.

Now we would like you to write down your primary love language on a piece of paper. Then put in rank order your remaining four languages. Once your lists are complete, compare them with each other. You may discover that your two primary languages rank least with your spouse, and vice versa. Discuss with your spouse what you will need to do to meet each other's needs in this area and how you will learn to speak their love language. Remember, it takes the missionaries in the Church about eight weeks at the Missionary Training Center and about another six months to a year to really learn a language well enough to communicate in a meaningful way. It may take that long, or even longer, to learn to communicate with a spouse in such a way that he or she feels understood.

Check Your Love Tanks

Before we discuss the ways we can learn to speak each other's love languages and fill each other's needs, consider the following idea. When one of the authors, Doug, teaches seminars or classes, he will often explain a quantitative method of ranking activities that couples can engage in. Specifically, he asks couples to rank their interest in activities on a scale of one to ten, one being the lowest and ten being the highest. This is an effective way to help with decision making. How many times have you and your spouse done something together only to find out later that neither of you really wanted to participate in the activity? Couples, ourselves included, have been to dinners, movies, vacations, and everything else in between only to find out later that one or the other partner never really wanted to participate in that activity or event in the first place.

How about a new technique? This time, you call your wife and say, "Honey, on a scale of one to ten, rate how important it would be to you to go out tonight." If she says, "I would put that at a nine and a half," then you'd better get a babysitter quickly. You're going out whether you want to or not. However, if she rates the activity about a five or less, then you could explain that you would rate it at about a two. Then you could both agree to do something else. For instance, you could say, "Honey, I was thinking that we stay home tonight, order a pizza, put the kids down early, and watch a movie together. What do you think about that?" She may say, "I'm thinking an eight." And then you could let her know that you are about a nine on that one.

The same principle applies to your love tank. We have used the analogy of a love *bank* before, but now we're talking about a love *tank*. Think of it as a gas tank, constantly being emptied and needing fuel. We invite you to check your love tanks often. When you come home every night this week, check the gauge on your spouse's love tank. Just ask, "Honey, how is your love tank tonight?" After your spouse gives you a reading, then make a suggestion. What is something that you could say or do to fill his or her tank? You could take turns. One night, the wife gets her tank filled, and the next night, it is the husband's turn.

Like a gas tank, you *could* push the limit and let the tank go empty, forcing your spouse to run on fumes, so to speak. But that is neither safe nor healthy for a car or a spouse. It is better for you to fill the tank often, making sure it is well above any dangerous level. Now, remember, you fill your spouse's tank by speaking his or her love language, not yours.

Love Is a Choice

The great news about all of this is that it is never too late to begin. You can start today. One of the authors, Mark, had been married about fifteen years when he discovered that he was speaking Mandarin and Janie was speaking Spanish. She was gift-oriented, and he wasn't giving her the greatest gift—the gift of presence. That's all she needed—just somebody to be there with her, someone to ride in the car with her to Wal-Mart, someone to paint a room with. At the same time, all he needed was for her to say, "Hey, you paint so well," or "Thanks for coming with me to Wal-Mart," or "Thanks for coming home early from work today to spend time with me."

Regardless of where we're at in our marriages, we can change. Love will not erase the past, but it can make the future different. Love helps create an emotional climate in which we can deal positively with what needs to change. We can slowly build and fortify our marriages beyond the harm of past mistakes. But this will take action. Meeting the love needs of our spouses is a choice. It is something that can be learned.

What if the love language of your spouse doesn't come naturally for you? The answer is, "Learn it." Many couples claim they have "fallen out of love." The couples who make this claim haven't really fallen out of love; they have simply quit nurturing the marriage.

Consider an applicable analogy Dr. Brent Barlow shared once:

> Susan and I learned this not long ago when we planted grass in our backyard. As it started to grow, so did the crab-grass. So many neighbors and friends told us about the crabgrass in our new lawn that we soon began to believe

the crabgrass would prevail. And for a while it did. The neighborhood consensus was that the lawn could not survive. Anyone could see that, just by looking at it! The crabgrass was so tall that the little blades of new lawn were barely visible.

One neighbor told us to simply start over. He showed us how to spray the yard with a chemical that would kill everything. Another neighbor offered us his tiller. We were discouraged, to say the least. It had taken us several months to get even this far with our new lawn. We'd had to dig up rocks, bring in topsoil, level, fertilize, and prepare the area for the lawn seed.

While we were trying to make a decision, I stopped by a greenhouse one day with a few blades of the crabgrass. I described our plight to an elderly man who looked like he knew something about plants and grass. "That's not crabgrass; it's orchard grass," he said. "Just give your lawn a little more water, fertilizer, and time. As the new lawn grows, it will soon crowd out the orchard grass." We followed his advice and now have a backyard of beautiful, thriving lawn.

Marriage also has its discouraging moments once in a while—a little unwanted crabgrass. And sometimes we may just want to give up the good in order to get rid of the bad. But the advice from the man at the nursery still seems pertinent. Give it a little more attention, make a little more effort, and the good experiences can eventually crowd out the bad ones. Focus your effort and attention on the lawn rather than on the crabgrass. [20]

We submit that couples do not fall out of love easily. They have simply quit weeding, watering, and fertilizing. It's not time to visit a lawyer; it's time to revisit the lawn. Don't give up something good for something worse. Hang in there! The Apostle Marvin J. Ashton declared:

We must at regular and appropriate intervals speak and reassure others of our love and the long time it takes to prove it by our actions. Real love does take time. The Great Shepherd had the same thoughts in mind when he taught, "If ye love me, *keep* my commandments" (see John 14:15) and "If ye love me *feed* my sheep" (see John 21:16). Love demands action if it is to be continuing. Love is a process. Love is not a declaration. Love is not an announcement. Love is not a passing fancy. Love is not an expediency. Love is not a convenience. "If ye love me, keep my commandments" and "If ye love me feed my sheep" are God-given proclamations that should remind us we can often best show our love through the processes of feeding and keeping.[21]

Conclusion

As we can see, loving someone and *showing* that love are two very different things. This difference is where true, deep communication comes into play. It is the difference between saying and doing. It is the difference between hypocrisy and sincerity. It is the difference between surviving and *thriving*. In learning *how* to love one another, we learn to put aside our selfishness and pride. We learn to put our spouse's needs first and to love them in ways that are appreciated by them.

CHAPTER 14

the marriage triad

Now we come to the center of it all. We've worked so hard on ridding ourselves of selfishness and pride, and to what end? The satisfaction of a job well done? Hardly. Our purpose in all this is to strengthen our marriages, to become the marriage partners the Lord would have us be. That is when our marriages will truly be successful—when they are indeed sanctioned by the Lord. Once He becomes an approving partner in the marriage, there is really nothing that can undermine it. Unfortunately, far too many are forgetting this important aspect of marriage. They fail to see the need for God to join them together, and so see their marriages "put asunder" (see Matt. 19:6).

Recently, *USA Today* featured a front-page article about civil marriage in our country. The article stated that "fewer American couples who marry today see the need for religion's approval."[1] Put another way, there is a trend in our country to be married by civil authority rather than the clergy. In fact, more than 40% of marriages today are performed civilly rather than religiously.[2] Marriage is becoming more of a bond between husband and wife, with no acknowledgment of God's presence or blessing.

This trend perfectly depicts the larger problems in society today— gang activity, broken families, drug abuse, violent crime, child neglect, and apathy. The basic problem is that we have become a Godless society. This great nation that was founded on religious principles now condemns those who want to continue those same principles. And without a divine presence in our lives, without God in our families, we will not succeed. With Him, we have a chance.

Perhaps we could better emphasize this principle with a story. A few years ago, the Church aired a satellite broadcast hosted by Elder M. Russell Ballard of the Quorum of the Twelve Apostles. Elder Ballard interviewed prominent members of the Church regarding their testimonies of the gospel, personal experiences with the scriptures, and feelings about the Savior. One of the experiences shared that evening came from the life of Wayne Osmond, of Osmond family fame.

Wayne explained that he had recently been diagnosed with a malignant brain tumor. Although the prognosis was grim, his faith, his wife's faith, and his children's faith in the Lord Jesus Christ is what pulled them through. Wayne further related to Elder Ballard that when he was on the gurney about to be wheeled into surgery, he held his wife's hand and said, "I love you, honey. Don't you worry, the Lord is with us." Wayne then shared this testimony: "If we didn't have that Rock to hold onto, where would we be? We'd just be floundering. We'd have nothing."[3]

Think of that statement. *If we didn't have that Rock to hold onto, where would we be?* Here was a man who some might think had it all—fame, fortune, and family. Yet, when it came right down to the bottom line, Wayne Osmond was saying that the most important thing in his life and in the life of his family was the Savior Jesus Christ and the principles of the gospel. Moreover, if his family did not have that *Rock*, they would truly be nothing. And so it is with each of us.

Jesus Christ Is the Sure Foundation

Matthew 7:24–27 tells of two men, one wise and one foolish. The wise man built his house upon a solid foundation, a rock. When the rains fell and the floods came and the winds blew, his house (and his family) stood strong. On the contrary, when the storm came upon the foolish man's household, the one who built his house upon the sand (or a much less stable foundation), he lost all he had. It is that simple: put Christ at the center of your life, and you'll live—don't, and you'll die. It was President Howard W. Hunter who declared, "Please remember this one thing. If our lives . . . are centered upon Jesus Christ . . . nothing can ever go permanently wrong. On the other hand, if our lives are not centered on the Savior and his teachings, no other success can be permanently right."[4] In Helaman 5:12, we are taught:

> And now, my sons, remember, remember that it is upon the rock of our Redeemer, who is Christ, the Son of God, that ye must build your foundation; that when the devil shall send forth his mighty winds, yea, his shafts in the whirlwind, yea, when all his hail and his mighty storm shall beat upon you, it shall have no power over you to drag you down to the gulf of misery and endless wo, because of the rock upon which ye are built, which is a sure foundation, a foundation whereon if men build they cannot fall.

As our focus in this book is marriage, consider the temple. The majestic Salt Lake Temple stands squarely in the center of Salt Lake City. In fact, the entire city was built around the temple. The streets are numbered according to where they stand in relationship to the temple; a person's address can tell them where their home stands in relation to the temple. The temple is a symbol of the Savior. Just as Temple Square is the geographic center of Salt Lake City, so should the Savior be at the center of each of our lives and marriages. Such centering gives us clearer perspective in marriage; we will come to see each other as He does. C. S. Lewis once said, "I believe in [Christ] as I believe that the sun has risen, not only because I see it, but because by it I see everything else."[5] To center our marriages on the Savior is to see them and each other through His eyes, to walk through life with His feet, to care for each other with His hands, to say what He would say and do what He would do.

Another important concept taught in the previous verse from Helaman reminds us that the devil is after us. He is after our marriages. It is not a matter of *if* he will attack, but *when*. But this passage of scripture also suggests that, regardless of what Satan tries to do to us, he will have no power over us if we are centered in the

Savior. Joseph Smith taught, "The devil has no power over us only as we permit him."⁶ Certainly, Satan can have no power over us if our lives are built on the Rock, which is Christ.

Relationships Built on a Sure Foundation

From the proclamation on the family we learn that "Happiness in family life is most likely to be achieved when founded upon the teachings of the Lord Jesus Christ."⁷ If your marriage relationship is built on the Savior and His teachings, you will be happy and successful. In a general conference address, President Howard W. Hunter reminded us that "whatever Jesus lays his hands upon lives."⁸ President Hunter added that if Jesus lays His hands on a marriage, it will live. Likewise, if Jesus lays His hands upon a family or a husband or wife, they will live. That is, they will thrive, they will grow, they will develop, they will heal, and they will succeed.

What does it mean to have a marriage built on the foundation of Christ? Such a marriage can be characterized as a couple who pray together regularly to call down upon them the blessings of heaven and who consistently read from good Church literature, including the scriptures and Church magazines, and strive to apply what they learn. When President Thomas S. Monson and his wife Frances were sealed in the Salt Lake Temple years ago, Benjamin Bowring offered the following counsel:

> May I offer you newlyweds a formula which will ensure that any disagreement you may have will last no longer than one day? Every night kneel by the side of your bed. One night, Brother Monson, you offer the prayer, aloud, on bended knee. The next night, you, Sister Monson, offer the prayer, aloud, on bended knee. I can then assure you that any misunderstanding that develops during the day will vanish as you pray. You simply can't pray together and retain any but the best of feelings toward one another.⁹

Why is this so? Because in praying, we draw ourselves closer to the Lord. We make Him a part of our marriage, and, as stated above, we see situations and each other with true perspective. We are filled with the Spirit and with His love. It was President David O. McKay who declared: "I regard it as an incontrovertible fact that in no marriage circle can true peace, love, purity, chastity, and happiness be found, in which is not present the Spirit of Christ, and the daily, hourly striving after loving obedience to his divine commands, and especially the nightly prayer expressing gratitude for blessings received."[10]

A couple who has built their foundation on the Savior also serve in the Church and assist their fellow beings. They have stripped themselves of pride and envy, and they seek to put each other's needs before their own. President Spencer W. Kimball described such a couple this way: "When a husband and wife go together frequently to the holy temple, kneel in prayer together in their home with their family, go hand in hand to their religious meetings, keep their lives wholly chaste, mentally and physically, . . . and both are working together for the upbuilding of the kingdom of God, then happiness is at its pinnacle."[11]

As we have worked with many struggling couples over the years, we feel comfortable estimating that over 90% of the couples we have visited with did *not* follow President Kimball's counsel. They were *not* attending the temple; they were *not* attending their religious meetings; they were *not* living wholly chaste lives; they were *not* working together in building the kingdom as they served their families (first) and the Church. Consequently, they were *not* happy. Yes, initially the Savior was a part of their marriage; initially they were following President Kimball's counsel and living the gospel. They *started* their marriage with the temple. But for some reason, that all changed. For some reason, they shut off the flow of the Spirit, and subsequently, the lifeblood of their marriage evaporated. Marriages need not be as such. The good news is that if your marriage is off track, you can change. You can put things back together. You can invite the Savior back into your lives and into your marriage by doing that which He commands us to do. He can heal you and your marriage, and He can bless you again as He did in the beginning of your relationship.

Common Distractions

Centering your lives on Christ is not as simple as it sounds. There will always be distractions. In Stephen R. Covey's book, *The Divine Center*, he speaks of these distractions, or, as he labels them, distortions. These distortions, ironically, are the very things from which we seek happiness, security, wisdom, guidance, and power. Two of these distortions apply to many Latter-day Saints. We become either spouse-centered or Church-centered.

The Spouse-Centered Life

This caution may seem strange, since the focus of our book has been marriage. But being thus centered, basing all our purpose and chance for happiness on our spouse, is unhealthy. Despite the fact that the husband-wife dyad is one of the central relationships in the kingdom of God and will eventually be the focal relationship in the celestial kingdom (our children will be with their own spouses), we warn against overdependence. Covey describes it this way: "When a person's sense of emotional worth comes primarily from the marriage relationship, then he or she becomes highly dependent upon that relationship. That makes him or her extremely vulnerable to the moods and feelings, the behavior and treatment, of the partner, and to any external event which may impinge the relationship—a new child, in-laws, economic setbacks, social successes, and so forth."[12]

Please do not misunderstand. We are not saying not to love your spouse too much. We should love our spouses deeply and do everything in our power to nurture the marriage relationship daily. Doctrine and Covenants 42:22 states: "Thou shalt love thy wife with all thy heart, and shalt cleave unto her and none else." Cleaving suggests loyalty and faithfulness. But *cleaving* is not *clinging*. Nor is it meant to imply that we dominate our spouse's time or isolate him or her from others.

Remember, your spouse was one of Heavenly Father's sons or daughters before he or she became your spouse. It would be wrong to think of keeping one's spouse all to oneself. Your spouse is a child of Heavenly Father and has a mission to perform on this earth. No marriage partner should stand in the way of that; instead, we should help our spouses fulfill their missions however we can.

Occasionally we meet a husband who is possessive of his wife and who seems to feel that the wife's mission in life to is serve him and be there for him all of the time. We know of one man who expects a four-course meal to be served for dinner every night promptly when he comes home from work. If his wife chooses not to do it or forgets because she is preoccupied or has another commitment, he makes her pay for her mistake. He gets grumpy when he isn't fed. We know of another man who has a very social wife with many friends in her ward. However, he doesn't think that he should have to share his wife with other Church members. While men like this place all the responsibility for personal happiness on their wives, some women also unhealthily derive all their identity and worth from their husbands.

Another caution when it comes to spouse-centeredness is a spouse who seems to worship the other. We are aware of a husband and wife who could be in this danger. This particular couple have been married for some time, and still, like newlyweds, their entire world revolves around each other. Aside from the way they continually talk baby talk to each other, the wife often takes time in testimony meeting to share how her husband is the greatest man in the world. She can be found at Church softball games cheering wildly for him as he rounds the bases, holding up a sign she made at ward enrichment that says something like, "Way to Go, Jim. You Are the Greatest Ball Player in the Church!" Although I think many people would admire this couple's relationship, there are red flags here. Obsession is unhealthy.

What Stephen Covey says is true. When a partner's sense of meaning and worth is derived from his or her spouse, he or she becomes highly dependent on the partner. It certainly places a faithful and trusting spouse in a vulnerable position. For example, if a wife is wholly dependent on her husband and the husband fails (either he dies or leaves the marriage), what is there left for the wife? She has put her entire strength and devotion for the last several years into a relationship that will not yield dividends. In fact, forget death or an affair; let's just say he gets busy with work and Church affairs and cannot give her back what she is giving him. She will undoubtedly feel slighted and frustrated, and it could get worse from there.

Doctrine and Covenants 42:22 does say that we should love our *spouse* with all of our hearts. However, there is one higher law that applies, and that is Matthew 22:37, which teaches us that we should love *God* with all of our hearts, souls, and minds. When we put God at the center of our lives and love Him more than we love anyone else, it increases our capacity to love others. That is, we can love our spouse more deeply and profoundly when we love God first. Why? Because God *is* love (see 1 John 4:8), and when we love Him first, He blesses us with an endowment—the gift of charity. He places within us a power to love our spouse, children, and neighbors the very way He loves us. Without that gift, we are left on our own to love, and that could be dangerous. We are weak, and those around us are weak. Without God's help, we may be too judgmental or too darn cranky to purely love our families and fellow beings.

The Church-Centered Life

Another very important aspect in our lives is the Church. "How can this take me *away* from being Christ-centered?" you might ask. The Church is supposed to bring us closer to the Lord, right? Yes, that is the purpose of the Church, and it's important, just as marriage and our spouse are. But again, we must not get so caught up in the administration and organization that we miss what it's all pointing to. Covey explains:

> [The] Church is a means to an end, not an end in itself. The Church is the instrument. It is the vehicle, the conveyer, having the three-fold mission and role. . . . But by itself it cannot be a person's effective center, because it is itself dependent. . . . It is of critical importance that we see the Church as a means to an end and not an end in itself. Most members of the Church know in their hearts that there is a very clear and distinct difference between being active in the Church and being active in the gospel. . . . There are Church-centered people who escape from the more rigorous responsibilities in the marriage and the family by saying, "I'm going to do the work of the Church"

(or "the work of the kingdom," or "the work of the Lord"). Attending meetings, interviewing others regarding their own worthiness, or conducting worthwhile programs for others may be much easier than confronting and solving a difficult emotional situation at home with the spouse or the teenage son or daughter. Sometimes such a member, of whatever leadership position, will fully rationalize family neglect [in] the name of the Church.[13]

The warning from Covey is clear. Don't get so caught up in "building the kingdom" that you neglect the most important people of all—your spouse and children. President Harold B. Lee commented on this problem, especially with husbands and fathers:

> Sometimes as I go throughout the Church, I think I am seeing a man who is using his church work as a kind of escape from family responsibility. And sometimes when we've talked about whether or not he's giving attention to his family, his children and his wife, he says something like this: "Well, I'm so busy taking care of the Lord's work that I really don't have time." And I say to him, "My dear brother, the greatest of the Lord's work that you and I will ever do is the work that we do within the walls of our own home." Now don't you get any misconception about where the Lord's work starts. That's the most important of the Lord's work. And you wives may have to remind your husbands of that occasionally.[14]

There must be a healthy balance. We must not let even these important elements distract us from our focus. As we become Christ-centered, we become like Him—and our priorities fall into place.

The Christ-Centered Marriage

Now, if Christ is our focus in our individual lives, consider the strength this center can be to our marriages. The Lord's power can strengthen and unify people in a way that nothing else can. Covey further explained this principle in terms of how it changes our vision:

> When a person has this map or frame of reference, the Lord and his work become the driving force of that person's life. It becomes the unifying and organizational principle, the center around which everything revolves. . . . In keeping with Christ's example, if the God/Christ-centered person is offended, he blesses in return. He returns kindness for unkindness, patience for impatience. If he is afflicted, he chooses a response which enables him to grow and learn from the affliction, to suffer with meaning and nobility, a response which will have a greater influence on others than perhaps any other value. . . . If the person is praised, he gives thanks. If he is blamed, he appraises the matter to see whether there may be some blameworthiness in him, and if there is, he plans self-improvement. But he does not overreact and either accuse or blame in return, or condemn himself. . . . [Instead] he seeks to identify with Christ. Christ is his model. For instance, he studies scriptural accounts of the Savior's earthly life, and as he does so he visualizes each of the situations recorded. He empathizes with the people involved, sees himself as part of the action, feels himself in the more positive, disciple-type roles. He creates in his mind his response to present-day situations based on living by the principles represented by the scriptural accounts. . . . Gradually, as he comes to see the Savior as the perfect model and mentor, he identifies with that mental image and vision. In this way he acquires "the mind of Christ" and thus gradually learns to respond to life situations as [Christ] would have responded.[15]

Seeing the world through the Savior's eyes, walking where He would walk, saying what He would say, and touching those He would touch—that is what one does who lives a life centered on the Savior. Now, imagine two people, so centered, being unified in marriage.

Could such a marriage fail? Paul exhorted the Corinthian Saints to possess the "mind of Christ" (1 Cor. 2:16). Elder Bruce R. McConkie explained that having the mind of Christ is "to believe what He believes, think what He thinks, say what He says, and do what He does. It is to be one with Him by the power of the Holy Ghost."[16] Our thoughts govern our behaviors; by changing our thoughts, we can have the power to change our behaviors. If our thoughts are centered on the Savior, we obtain the power to behave like the Savior. Think of how the world would be different if married couples possessed the mind of the Savior. Think of how many marriages would be healed.

A few years ago, after an Education Week presentation, Dr. Brent Barlow told us that a young man and his wife approached him and asked if they could talk to him. The man, in his early thirties, was a member of the Church who was a successful executive. He told of how, in his recent past, he had often worked sixty to seventy hours per week while ignoring his wife and new baby. His job had also required him to travel a great deal during the week and on weekends. So, besides not spending time with his family, he'd been missing church as well. Dr. Barlow related:

> At first he tried to attend church at wards in the cities where he had to conduct business, but after a time he stopped making the effort. He became involved with a woman colleague at his office, spending a great deal of time with her. At first the relationship was supposedly businesslike and professional, but then they became emotionally attached to each other. A sexual encounter loomed as a likely possibility. Then, about the time he was promoted to the high-salaried position he was aspiring to, his wife filed for divorce.
>
> The young executive said he made several attempts at reconciliation. He reluctantly agreed to see their bishop, who suggested that they needed professional counseling. That avenue was pursued but to no avail—the damage had apparently been done. They finally entered the waiting period before their divorce would be final.

The husband became a little tearful as he continued his story. He realized that he would lose his young wife by divorce and that subsequently his relationship with his little daughter would be limited. The divorce and final separation seemed inevitable.

So he made a decision. As a priesthood holder and returned missionary, he still wanted to retain his membership in the Church and reestablish his relationship with the Savior. In essence, he decided not so much to "come unto Christ" as to "return to Christ." During the few weeks before the finalization of the divorce, he began praying alone and fasting periodically. He stopped seeing and traveling with the woman at his office. He attended his priesthood and other Church meetings regularly for the first time in several months. He started to study the gospel and get more involved in Church service. He examined his heart and tried to bring spirituality into his life. He did all these things fully expecting that his wife and child would soon leave him. But unknown to him, his wife was observing him. (As he was telling me about this episode in their lives, she was holding onto his arm, also in tears.)

The wife then continued the story. She said she noted some sincere and genuine changes in him as he tried drawing closer to the Lord. When the time came for her to sign the final divorce papers, she called her attorney and said that she was going to delay the action another thirty days.

The husband made major adjustments with his employment, even taking a cut in pay. He had realized the significance of the statement, "For what is a man profited, if he shall gain the whole world, and lose his own soul [and wife and daughter]? or what shall a man give in exchange for his soul?" (Matthew 16:26.) By the time the thirty days was up, the wife had decided not to sign the divorce papers.[17]

There is a tremendous power in the gospel of Jesus Christ. God can heal and strengthen your family relationships. In Matthew 25:40 we read, "Inasmuch as ye have done it unto one of the least of these my brethren, ye have done it unto me." We call this the platinum rule. In the context of marriage, we are each to treat our spouse as if he or she were the Savior, or as the Savior would treat him or her. Although this is a lofty ideal, it should be something we seriously consider and then put into practice. It is a celestial law. All who live it will reap celestial rewards.

When couples fail to center their relationship on the teachings of the Master, they have no promise or guarantee that things will work out. In fact, they do not even have the resources to correct their course. Without the Lord's Spirit, the power to be kind and compassionate is almost impossible. The natural man takes over in most cases. Human kindness and charity wane when spiritual resources are ignored or forgotten, and a relationship deteriorates. Individuals without the Spirit become sarcastic, angry, critical, defensive, and uncaring. On the other hand, when we understand the eternal purpose of marriage, the Savior is a part of the relationship, and then we succeed as we become more like Him.

Conclusion

The time to put Christ at the center of your life is right now. A Christ-centered approach can successfully drive all of the marriage and family decisions you will make. The Savior's love will nurture and anchor your personality and character so that you will not allow Satan to influence your marriage.

As with the couple in the story Dr. Barlow related, if we put the Savior at the center of our lives, He will take care of each of us. And He will help us take care of each other. Whatever He puts His hand on will live. Whatever He touches will thrive.

All personal quotes not cited are from our clients and students who were gracious enough to allow the use of such to help others. We appreciate their consideration in this endeavor.

NOTES FOR INTRODUCTION

1. These ideas come from William J. Doherty's keynote address at the Smart Marriage Conference, 21 June 2001, Orlando, Florida. WWW.smartmarriages.com/citizen.marriage.html
2. Ibid.
3. Ibid.
4. Arlie R. Hochschild, "How Has 'The Organization Man' Aged: A Need to Belong," *The New York Times,* 17 Jan. 1999, 17; emphasis added.
5. *The State of Our Unions: The Social Health of Marriage in America. The National Marriage Project* (New Jersey: Rutgers University Press, 2003), 31.
6. Cited in Brent A. Barlow, "Marriage at the Crossroads," *Marriage and Families,* Jan. 2003, 22.
7. David B. Haight, "Marriage and Divorce," *Ensign,* May 1984, 12–13.
8. "Marital Stress Hammers Wives," *USA Today*, 21 June 2001, 8D.
9. Brent A. Barlow, "Marriage at the Crossroads," *Marriage and Families,* Jan. 2003, 23–24.
10. Karen S. Peterson, "The Good in a Bad Marriage," *USA Today,* 21 June 2001, 8D.
11. Brent A. Barlow, "Marriage at the Crossroads," *Marriage and Families,* Jan. 2003, 23.
12. http://enrichmentjournal.ag.org/200003/030_too_large.cfm, 15 June 2003.
13. "The Family: A Proclamation to the World," *Ensign,* Nov. 1995, 102.
14. Cited in Bob Mims, "Mormons: High Conservativism, Low Divorce, Big Growth," *Salt Lake Tribune,* 6 Mar. 1999. Internet Transcript: http://archives.his.com/smartmarriages/msg00683.html.

15. Harold B. Lee, *Teachings of Harold B. Lee* (Bookcraft: Salt Lake City, 1996), 277.

16. Gordon B. Hinckley, "Walking in the Light of the Lord," *Ensign*, Nov. 1998, 99.

17. www.heritage.org/research/features/marriage/explanation.ctg, Heritage Foundation, *The Positive Effects of Marriage: A Book of Charts, Chart 14: Marriage and Personal Happiness*, 1998.

18. Elizabeth VanDenBerghe, "The Enduring, Happy Marriage: Findings and Implications from Research," *Strengthening Our Families* (Salt Lake City: Bookcraft, 2000), 20.

19. James E. Faust, "The Enriching of Marriage," *Ensign*, Nov. 1977, 10.

CHAPTER 1 NOTES

1. Boyd K. Packer. *Ensign*, May 2004, 20.

2. Joseph F. Smith, *CR*, April 1913, 118.

3. Henry B. Eyring, "That We May Be One," *Ensign*, May 1998, 66.

4. Linda Wait, "Marriage Matters," *Demography*, Nov. 1995, 483–507.

5. Richard G. Scott, "The Joy of Living the Great Plan of Happiness," *Ensign*, Nov. 1996, 73–74.

6. Cited in Brent A. Barlow, *What Wives Expect of Husbands* (Salt Lake City: Deseret Book, 1989), 104.

7. Howard W. Hunter, "Follow the Son of God," *Ensign*, Nov. 1994, 87.

8. Spencer W. Kimball, *Faith Precedes the Miracle* (Salt Lake City: Deseret Book, 1972), 130–31.

9. Ezra Taft Benson, *Come, Listen to a Prophet's Voice* (Salt Lake City: Deseret Book, 1990), 54.

10. Howard W. Hunter, *CR*, Oct. 1994, 68.

11. Marvin K. Gardner, Don L. Searle, "At Home with the Hinckleys," *Ensign*, Oct. 2003, 22.

12. Marlin K. Jensen, "A Union of Love and Understanding," *Ensign*, Oct. 1994, 51.

13. Debbi Kiss, *Meridian Magazine*, www.meridianmagazine.com/familyconnections/030214lovestories2.html, 27 Dec. 2004.

14. Jeffrey R. Holland, *On Earth As It Is in Heaven* (Salt Lake City: Deseret Book, 1989), 109–10; italics added.
15. Stephen L Richards, *CR*, Apr. 1949, 136.
16. Spencer W. Kimball, *Marriage and Divorce* (Salt Lake City: Deseret Book, 1976), 24.

CHAPTER 2 NOTES

1. "The Family: A Proclamation to the World." *Ensign*, Nov. 1995, 102.
2. Robert E. Wells, "Overcoming Those Differences of Opinion," *Ensign*, Jan. 1987, 61–62.
3. *The Teachings of Spencer W. Kimball*, ed. Edward L. Kimball (Salt Lake City: Bookcraft, 1982), 313.
4. Ezra Taft Benson, *CR*, Apr. 1989, 6–7.
5. George Gallup Jr. and Frank Newport, "Time at a Premium for Many Americans," *Gallup Poll Monthly*, Nov. 1990, 45.
6. Michael McClean, "Are You Giving the Least?" *Together Forever* (Salt Lake City: Bonneville Media Communications, 1988).
7 . Cited in Robert L. Millett, *Alive in Christ* (Salt Lake City: Deseret Book, 1997), 52.
8. Jeffrey R. Holland, *However Long and Hard the Road* (Salt Lake City: Deseret Book, 1985), 6.
9. C. Richard Chidister, *Eternal Companions* (Salt Lake City: Bookcraft, 1995), 22–23.
10. Ezra Taft Benson, *CR*, Apr. 1989, 6.
11. Jeffrey R. Holland, *However Long and Hard the Road* (Salt Lake City: Deseret Book, 1985), 6.
12. Cited in David O. McKay, "Salvation, An Individual Responsibility," *Improvement Era*, June 1957, 391.
13. Bruce R. McConkie, *Church News*, 24 Jan. 1976, 4.
14. Boyd K. Packer, *CR*, Oct. 1986, 20.
15. Howard W. Hunter, "Come Unto Me," *Ensign*, Nov. 1990, 18.
16. Howard W. Hunter, "God Will Have a Tried People" *Ensign*, Nov. 1979, 65.
17. Boyd K. Packer, *Problems in Teaching the Moral Standard* (address delivered at seminary and institute faculty summer school, Brigham Young University, 15 July 1958), 10–11.

18. Cited in Victor L. Brown, "The Vision of the Aaronic Priesthood," *Ensign*, Nov. 1975, 66.

19. Ezra Taft Benson, "To the Fathers in Israel," *Come, Listen to a Prophet's Voice* (Salt Lake City: Deseret Book, 1990), 43–44.

20. Yoshihiko Kikuchi, "Daughter of God," *Ensign*, May 1988, 76–77.

CHAPTER 3 NOTES

1. Adapted from H. Norman Wright, *More Communication Keys for Your Marriage* (Ventura, Calif. Regal Books, 1983) and Brent A. Barlow, *Dealing with Differences in Marriage* (Salt Lake City: Deseret Book, 1993), 29.

2. Jeffrey R. and Patricia T. Holland, "Some Things We Have Learned—Together," *On Earth As It Is in Heaven* (Salt Lake City: Deseret Book, 1989), 103–4.

3. Joyce Brothers, *What Every Woman Should Know about Men* (New York: Simon and Schuster, 1981), 11, 39–40.

4. James Dobson, *Bringing Up Boys* (Wheaton, Ill.: Tyndale House Publishers, 2001), 16.

5. Ibid., 25.

6. H. Norman Wright, *More Communication Keys for Your Marriage* (Ventura: Regal Books 1983), 123.

7. Jeff Foxworthy, *Jeff Foxworthy: Totally Committed* (New York: Home Box Office Home Video, 1998).

8. James Dobson, *Bringing Up Boys,* (Wheaton, Ill.: Tyndale House Publishers, 2001), 23.

9. Gary Smally seminar, personal notes of author, Feb. 1989.

10. National Council of Family Relations, Milwaukee, Wisconsin, personal notes of author, Nov. 1998.

11. John Gray, *Men Are from Mars, Women Are from Venus* (New York: HarperCollins, 1992), 29.

12. "The Family: A Proclamation to the World," *Ensign*, Nov. 1995, 102.

13. David Popenoe, *Life without Father* (New York: Martin Kessler Books, 1996)

14. Joe J. Christensen, *One Step at a Time* (Salt Lake City: Deseret Book, 1996), 25.

15. Brent A. Barlow, *Dealing with Differences in Marriage* (Salt Lake City: Deseret Book, 1993), 62.

16. Carlfred Broderick, *Couples* (New York: Simon and Schuster, 1979), 72–73.

17. James Dobson, *Bringing Up Boys* (Wheaton, Ill.: Tyndale House Publishers, 2001), 27.

18. *The Teachings of Spencer W. Kimball,* ed. Edward L. Kimball (Salt Lake City: Bookcraft, 1982), 315.

CHAPTER 4 NOTES

1. R. Wayne Pace, *Organizational Communication: Foundations for Human Resource Development* (Englewood Cliffs, N.J.: Prentice-Hall, Inc., 1983), 200.

2. Spencer W. Kimball, "The Privilege of Holding the Priesthood," *Priesthood* (Salt Lake City: Deseret Book, 1981), 4–5.

3. Gary Smalley, *Making Love Last Forever* (Dallas: Word Publishing, 1996), 253.

4. John Gottman, *Why Marriages Succeed or Fail ...*" (New York: Simon and Schuster, 1994), 57.

CHAPTER 5 NOTES

1. Willard. F. Harley, *His Needs, Her Needs* (Grand Rapids, Mich.: Fleming H. Revell, 2001), 49.

2. Ibid., 49–50.

3. Brent A. Barlow, *What Husbands Expect of Wives* (Salt Lake City: Desert Book, 1989), 53.

4. Richard G. Scott, *CR*, Apr. 2000, 47.

5. Joe J. Christensen, "Resolutions" *Ensign,* Dec. 1994, 62.

6. Jerome Chodorov, James B. Simpson, ed. *Contemporary Quotations* (New York: Cromwell Co., 1964), 238.

7. James Dobson, *Bringing Up Boys* (Wheaton, Ill.: Tyndale House Publishers, 2001), 23.

CHAPTER 6 NOTES

1. Willard F. Harley, *His Needs, Her Needs* (Grand Rapids, Mich: Fleming H. Revell, 2001), 60.
2. C. M. Musco Garcia-Prats and J. A. Garcia-Prats, *Good Marriages Don't Just Happen* (Allen, Tex.: Thomas Moore, 2000), 136–37.
3. Willard F. Harley, *His Needs, Her Needs* (Grand Rapids, Mich.: Fleming H. Revell, 2001), 40.
4. Gary Smalley, *Making Love Last Forever* (Dallas: Word Publishing, 1996), 141–42.
5. Cited in Brent Barlow, *Twelve Traps in Today's Marriage and How to Avoid Them* (Salt Lake City: Deseret Book, 1986), 82–83.
6. Willard F. Harley, *His Needs, Her Needs* (Grand Rapids, Mich.: Fleming H. Revell, 2001), 82.
7. N. Eldon Tanner, "Integrity," *Ensign*, May 1977, 16.
8. Bell, R.A., Daly, J.A., and Gonzalez, M.C. "Affinity-maintenance in marriage and its relationship to women's marital satisfaction." *Journal of Marriage and the Family* (1987), 49, 445–454.
9. Cited in F. Phillip Rice, *Intimate Relationships, Marriages, and Families* (Mountain View, Calif.: Mayfield Publishing, 1999), 241.
10. Marion D. Hanks, "Eternal Marriage," *Ensign*, Nov. 1984, 37.
11. Cited in Joe J. Christensen, *One Step at a Time* (Salt Lake City: Deseret Book, 1996), 43.
12. N. Eldon Tanner, "Constancy Amid Change," *Ensign*, Nov. 1979, 81.
13. "The Family: A Proclamation to the World," *Ensign*, Nov. 1995, 102.
14. Willard F. Harley, *His Needs, Her Needs* (Grand Rapids, Mich.: Fleming H. Revell, 2001), 82.
15. Neal A. Maxwell, *That My Family Should Partake* (Salt Lake City: Deseret Book, 1974), 16.
16. Ezra Taft Benson, "To the Fathers in Israel," *Ensign*, Nov. 1987, 50.
17. Howard W. Hunter, "Being a Righteous Husband and Father," *Ensign,* Nov. 1994, 49.

CHAPTER 7 NOTES

1. Jeffrey R. Holland, "Look to God and Live," *Ensign*, Nov. 1993, 13.
2. "Witnesses to Hockey Dad: 'You're Going to Kill Him,'" *cnn.com/Law Center* (posted 8 January 2002. See also "Hockey Dad Says He Fought in Defense," *Dallas Morning News*, 10 January 2002, 4A).
3. Cited in Carol Tavris, *Anger, the Misunderstood Emotion* (New York: Simon and Schuster, 1989), 164.
4. Michael Fumento, "'Road Rage' versus Reality," *The Atlantic Monthly*, Vol. 282, No. 2, 12–17.
5. Gordon B. Hinckley, "President Hinckley Notes His 85th Birthday, Reminisces About Life," *Church News*, 24 June 1995, 6; italics added.
6. Cited in Brent A. Barlow, *Twelve Traps in Today's Marriage and How to Avoid Them* (Salt Lake City: Deseret Book, 1986), 127.
7. Adapted from Lynn G. Robbins, "Agency and Anger," *Ensign*, May 1998, 80.
8. Gary Smalley, *Making Love Last Forever* (Dallas: Word Publishing, 1996), 20.
9. Carlfred Broderick, *One Flesh, One Heart* (Salt Lake City: Deseret Book, 1986), 40–41.
10. ElRay L. Christiansen, "Be Slow to Anger," *Ensign*, June 1971, 37–38.
11. Brent A. Barlow, *What Wives Expect of Husbands* (Salt Lake City: Deseret Book, 1989), 13.
12. Gordon B. Hinckley, "Women of the Church," *Ensign*, Nov. 1996, 68.
13. David O. McKay, comp. Llewelyn McKay, *Stepping Stones to an Abundant Life* (Salt Lake City: Deseret Book, 1971), 294.
14. Burton Kelly, "The Case Against Anger," *Ensign*, Febr. 1980, 8.
15. Cited in Steven R. Covey, *Spiritual Roots of Human Relations* (Salt Lake City: Deseret Book, 1970), 190–91.
16. Adapted from Lynn G. Robbins, "Agency and Anger," *Ensign*, May 1998, 80.
17. Richard L. Evans, comp. Richard L. Evans Jr., *Richard L. Evans: The Man and the Message* (Salt Lake City: Bookcraft, 1973), 301.

18. Richard Mower, *Overcoming Depression* (Salt Lake City: Deseret Book, 1986), 129–30.

19. *Discourses of Brigham Young*, sel. John A. Widtsoe (Salt Lake City: Deseret Book, 1941), 265.

20. Gordon B. Hinckley, "Make Marriage a Partnership," *Ensign*, Apr. 1984, 76.

21. Gordon B. Hinckley, "Except the Lord Build the House ..." *Ensign*, June 1971, 72.

22. Cited in Steven R. Covey, *Spiritual Roots of Human Relations* (Salt Lake City: Deseret Book, 1970), 113.

23. Stephen R. Covey and Truman G. Madsen, *Marriage and Family: Gospel Insights* (Salt Lake City: Bookcraft, 1983), 150–51.

24. *Discourses of Brigham Young*, sel. John A. Widtsoe (Salt Lake City: Deseret Book, 1941), 267.

25. Brigham Young, *Teachings of Presidents of the Church: Brigham Young* (Salt Lake City: The Church of Jesus Christ of Latter-day Saints, 1997), 166.

26. Gordon B. Hinckley, "The Continuing Pursuit of Truth," *Ensign*, Apr. 1986, 2–4.

27. Gordon B. Hinckley, *Teachings of Gordon B. Hinckley* (Salt Lake City: Deseret Book, 1997), 329.

28. *Hymns of The Church of Jesus Christ of Latter-day Saints* (Salt Lake City: Deseret Book, 1985), 336.

CHAPTER 8 NOTES

1. Victor L. Brown, *Human Intimacy* (Salt Lake City: Parliament, 1981), 135–36.

2. P. J. Knudsen and W. W. Knudsen, *Intimate Marriage: Toward Exultant Ecstasy* (Mesa, Az.: Institute for Marriage and Family Enrichment, 1992), 1.

3. *The Teachings of Spencer W. Kimball*, ed. Edward L. Kimball (Salt Lake City: Bookcraft, 1982), 312.

4. A. Burns, "Perceived Causes of Marriage Breakdown and the Conditions of Life," *Journal of Marriage and the Family*, 46, 551–62.

5. Elizabeth VanDenBerghe, "The Enduring, Happy Marriage: Findings and Implications from Research," *Strengthening Our Families: An In-Depth Look at the Proclamation on the Family*, ed. D. C. Dollahite (Salt Lake City: Deseret Book, 2000), 19.

6. Parley P. Pratt, *Key to the Science of Theology* (Salt Lake City: Deseret Book, 1965), 164.

7. Cited in Joseph Fielding Smith, *The Restoration of All Things* (Salt Lake City: Deseret Book, 1945), 261.

8. Jeffrey R. Holland and Patricia T. Holland, *On Earth As It Is in Heaven* (Salt Lake City: Deseret Book, 1989), 189–90.

9. *The Teachings of Spencer W. Kimball,* ed. Edward L. Kimball (Salt Lake City: Bookcraft, 1982), 312.

10. Kevin Leman, *Sex Begins in the Kitchen: Because Love Is an All-Day Affair* (Grand Rapids, Mich.: Baker Books, 1999).

11. Spencer W. Kimball, *Faith Precedes the Miracle* (Salt Lake City: Deseret Book, 1972), 130–31.

CHAPTER 9 NOTES

1. http://www.matrimonialbank.com/jokes.html

2. Lana Turner, http://www.brainyquote.com/quotes/authors/l/lana_turner .html

3. Cited in Joe J. Christensen, *One Step at a Time,* (Salt Lake City: Deseret Book, 1996), 43.

4. Marvin J. Ashton, *One for the Money: Guide to Family Finance* (Salt Lake City: Intellectual Reserve, 1992; pamphlet), 1.

5. Consumer Credit Counseling Service, "Money and Marriage: Don't Let Money Problems Ruin Your Relationship," http://www.cccsatl.org/money-marriage.asp

6. R.E. Berry and F.L. Williams, "Assessing the Relationships Between Quality of Life and Marital Income Satisfaction: A Path Analytic Approach," *Journal of Marriage and the Family*, cited in F.P. Rice, "Intimate Relationships," *Marriage and Families* (Mountain View, Calif.: Mayfield, 1996), 289.

7. Gordon B. Hinckley, *Cornerstones of a Happy Home* (Salt Lake City: Deseret Book, 1984), 8.

8. Marvin J. Ashton, *One for the Money: Guide to Family Finance* (Salt Lake City: Intellectual Reserve, 1992; pamphlet), 1.

9. Gordon B. Hinckley, "To the Boys and to the Men," *Ensign,* Nov. 1998, 53.

10. N. Eldon Tanner, "Constancy amid Change," *Ensign,* Nov. 1979, 81.

11. Ibid.

12. Janene Wolsey Baadsgaard, *Family Finances for the Flabbergasted* (Salt Lake City: Deseret Book, 1995), 41.

13. Brent A. Barlow, *Just for Newlyweds* (Salt Lake City: Deseret Book, 1992), 64–65; emphasis in original.

14. D. R. Mace, "Current Thinking on Marriage and Money," *Medical Aspects of Human Sexuality,* vol. 16, 109–18.

15. Joseph Smith, *Lectures on Faith* (Salt Lake City: Deseret Book, 1985), 38.

16. *Gospel Standards: Selections from the Sermons and Writings of Heber J. Grant, Seventh President of The Church of Jesus Christ of Latter-day Saints,* comp. G. Homer Durham (Salt Lake City: Deseret Book, 1981), 59.

17. Gordon B. Hinckley, "First Presidency Message: Inspirational Thoughts," *Ensign,* Aug. 1997, 7.

18. N. Eldon Tanner, "Constancy Amid Change," *Ensign,* Nov. 1979, 81.

19. Marvin J. Ashton, *One for the Money: Guide to Family Finance* (Salt Lake City: Intellectual Reserve, 1992; pamphlet), 6.

20. W. Steve Albrecht, "Making Money Your Ally," *Ensign,* Dec. 1988, 49.

21. Marvin J. Ashton, *One for the Money: Guide to Family Finance* (Salt Lake City: Intellectual Reserve, 1992; pamphlet), 1.

22. Joe J. Christensen, *One Step at a Time* (Salt Lake City: Deseret Book, 1996), 45.

23. B. O'Neill, *Financial Counseling and Planning Research Priorities, 1995–2000: A Practitioner's Viewpoint,* cited in R. Lytton, ed., *The Association for Financial Counseling and Planning Educational Proceedings* (Blacksburg, Va.: Virginia Polytech Institute and State University, 1994), 57–68.

24. Cited in C. Jathirtha and J. J. Fox, "Home Ownership and the Decision to Overspend," *Financial Counseling and Planning,* vol. 7, 1996, 57–69.

25. Jeffrey R. Holland, *However Long and Hard the Road* (Salt Lake City: Deseret Book, 1985), 106.

26. J. Reuben Clark, *CR,* Apr. 1938, 103.

27. Quoted in Shaun D. Stahle, "Tightening the Belt of Financial Extravagance," *Church News,* 29 Mar. 2003, 5.

28. Joe J. Christensen, "Greed, Selfishness, and Overindulgence," *Ensign,* May 1999, 9–10.

29. N. Eldon Tanner, "Constancy Amid Change," *Ensign,* Nov. 1979, 82.

CHAPTER 10 NOTES

1. Randal A. Wright, *A Case for Chastity* (USA: National Family Institute, 1993), 42.

2. Spencer W. Kimball, Regional Representatives' Seminar, 3 April 1974.

3. Gordon B. Hinckley, *Teachings of Gordon B. Hinckley* (Salt Lake City: Deseret Book, 1997), 172.

4. Victor B. Cline, *How to Make a Good Marriage Great: 10 Keys to a Joyous Relationship* (New York: Walker and Company, 1987), 59.

5. Cited in Jonathan Allen, "Physically Fit Marriage: Couples That Play Together, Stay Together," Dadstoday.com/resources/articles/fitnessmarriage.html, 16 May 2003.

6. Victor B. Cline, *How to Make a Good Marriage Great: 10 Keys to a Joyous Relationship* (New York: Walker and Company, 1987), 60.

7. Cited in L. Tom Perry, "If Ye Are Prepared, Ye Shall Not Fear," *Ensign,* Nov. 1995, 36.

8. Howard W. Hunter, "Prepare for Honorable Employment," *Ensign,* Nov. 1975, 122.

9. J. Thomas Fyans, "News of the Church," *Ensign,* May 1983, 84.

10. L. Tom Perry, "If Ye Are Prepared, Ye Shall Not Fear," *Ensign,* Nov. 1995, 36.

11. Ezra Taft Benson, "To the Fathers in Israel," *Ensign,* Nov. 1987, 49.

CHAPTER 11 NOTES

1. http://womencentral.net/marriage.html
2. Gordon B. Hinckley, *Teachings of Gordon B. Hinckley* (Salt Lake City: Deseret Book, 1997), 247–48.
3. Jeffrey R. Holland, "How Do I Love Thee?" *Brigham Young University Speeches, 1999–2000* (Provo: BYU) 159–60.

CHAPTER 12 NOTES

1. Cited in Doug E. Brinley, *Toward a Celestial Marriage* (Salt Lake City: Bookcraft, 1986), 97–99.
2. Robert E. Wells, "Overcoming Those Differences of Opinion," *Ensign*, Jan. 1987, 60.
3. Brent A. Barlow, *Just for Newlyweds* (Salt Lake City: Deseret Book, 1992), 36–38.
4. Boyd K. Packer, "Solving Emotional Problems in the Lord's Own Way," *Ensign*, May 1978, 93.
5. B. H. Roberts, *A Comprehensive History of the Church*, 1:131.
6. Spencer W. Kimball, *Marriage and Divorce* (Salt Lake City: Deseret Book, 1976), 13.
7. Diane Sollee, "Shifting Gears: An Optimistic View of the Future of Marriage," Conference on Communitarian Pro-Family Policies, Washington, D.C., 15 Nov. 1996, http://www.smart-marriages.com/optimistic.html
8. T. B. Holman, J. H. Larson, and R. F. Stahmann, "Preparing for an Eternal Marriage," *Strengthening Our Families: An In-Depth Look at the Proclamation on the Family* (Salt Lake City: Bookcraft, 2000), 39.
9. D. T. Seamons, "Ready or Not—Here We Are," in D. E. Brinley and D. K Judd, eds., *Eternal Companions* (Salt Lake City: Bookcraft, 1995), 123.
10. Delores Curran, *Stress and the Healthy Family* (New York: William Morrow & Company, 1993).
11. Ezra Taft Benson, "Salvation—A Family Affair," *Ensign*, July 1992, 2.
12. Adapted from Robert E. Wells, "Overcoming Those Differences of Opinion," *Ensign*, Jan. 1987, 61–62.

13. Gordon B. Hinckley, *CR*, Apr. 1971, 82.

14. *Teachings of Spencer W. Kimball,* ed. Edward L. Kimball (Salt Lake City: Bookcraft, 1982), 306–7.

CHAPTER 13 NOTES

1. Elizabeth Barrett Browning, *Sonnets from the Portuguese* [1850], no. 43.

2. Jeffrey R. Holland, "How Do I Love Thee?" *BYU Devotional and Fireside Speeches 1999–2000* (Provo: BYU), 158–59.

3. Hartman Rector Jr., "The Resurrection," *Ensign*, Nov. 1990, 77.

4. Jeffrey R. Holland, "How Do I Love Thee?" *BYU Devotional and Fireside Speeches 1999–2000* (Provo: BYU), 159.

5. Gary Chapman, *The Five Love Languages* (Chicago: Northfield Publishing, 1995), 221.

6. Joe J. Christensen, *One Step at a Time* (Salt Lake City: Deseret Book, 1996), 25.

7. Cited in Gary Chapman, *The Five Love Languages* (Chicago: Northfield Publishing, 1995), 39.

8. Gary Chapman, *The Five Love Languages* (Chicago: Northfield Publishing, 1995) 41–42.

9. Brent A. Barlow, "The Highs and Lows of Marriage," *Ensign*, October 1983, 44.

10. Gary Chapman, *The Five Love Languages* (Chicago: Northfield Publishing, 1995)

11. Ibid., 56.

12. Dee W. Hadley, "It Takes Time," *Ensign*, Dec. 1987, 29.

13. Gary Chapman, *The Five Love Languages* (Chicago: Northfield Publishing, 1995), 75.

14. Ibid., 79.

15. Brent A. Barlow, *Twelve Traps in Today's Marriage and How to Avoid Them* (Salt Lake City: Deseret Book, 1986), 56–57.

16. Gary Chapman, *The Five Love languages* (Chicago: Northfield Publishing, 1995), 88.

17. Gary L. Gray, "What I Learned about Serving My Wife," *Ensign*, June 1995, 56–57.

18. Gary Chapman, *The Five Love Languages* (Chicago: Northfield Publishing, 1995), 97.
19. Ibid., 104
20. Brent A. Barlow, "The Highs and Lows of Marriage," *Ensign*, Oct. 1983, 44.
21. Marvin J. Ashton, "Love Takes Time," *Ensign*, Nov. 1975, 108.

CHAPTER 14 NOTES

1. C. L. Grossman and I. S. Yoo, "Civil Marriage on Rise across USA," *USA Today*, 7 Oct. 2003, 1A.
2. Ibid.
3. "Witness of Christ: 1996 Missionary Open House," with Elder M. Russell Ballard of the Quorum of the Twelve Apostles. 25 February 1996 (Salt Lake City: Intellectual Reserve, 1997).
4. Howard W. Hunter, "Following the Master: Teachings of President Howard W. Hunter," *Ensign*, Apr. 1995, 21.
5. C. S. Lewis, "Is Theology Poetry?" in *The Weight of Glory and Other Addresses*, revised and expanded edition (New York: Macmillian, 1980), 92.
6. *Teachings of the Prophet Joseph Smith* (Salt Lake City: Deseret Book, 1979), 181.
7. "The Family: A Proclamation to the World," *Ensign*, Nov. 1995, 102.
8. Howard W. Hunter, *CR*, Oct. 1979, 93.
9. Quoted in Thomas S. Monson, "Hallmarks of a Happy Home," *Ensign*, Nov. 1988, 70.
10. David O. McKay, *Gospel Ideals* (Salt Lake City: Deseret Book, 1976), 473.
11. Spencer W. Kimball, *Marriage and Divorce* (Salt Lake City: Deseret Book, 1976), 24.
12. Stephen R. Covey, *The Divine Center* (Salt Lake City: Bookcraft, 1982), 23.
13. Ibid., 52–53.
14. Harold B. Lee, *Address to Seminary and Institute Personnel at Brigham Young University Summer School*, 8 July 1966.
15. Stephen R. Covey, *The Divine Center* (Salt Lake City: Bookcraft, 1982), 145, 148–49.

16. Bruce R. McConkie, *A New Witness for the Articles of Faith* (Salt Lake City: Deseret Book, 1985), 71.

17. Brent A. Barlow, *Dealing with Differences in Marriage* (Salt Lake City: Deseret Book, 1993), 121–23.